SPORTING DAYS

IN

SOUTHERN INDIA:

SPORTING DAYS

IN

SOUTHERN INDIA:

BEING
REMINISCENCES OF TWENTY TRIPS IN PURSUIT OF
BIG GAME, CHIEFLY IN THE MADRAS
PRESIDENCY.

BY

LIEUTENANT-COLONEL A.J. O. POLLOCK

GYAN

Published by

Gyan Publishing House
5, Ansari Road
Daryaganj, New Delhi-110002
Phone: 011-47034999, 9811692060
E-mail: books@gyanbooks.com

Distribution Network
gyanbooks.com
India, USA, Canada, UK, Australia

ISBN: 978-93-6280-927-8 (PB)
First Published, 1894

2nd Impression 2024

Printed at: Gyan Press, Delhi.

SPORTING DAYS IN SOUTHERN INDIA:
Author: LIEUTENANT-COLONEL A.J. O. POLLOCK

SPORTING DAYS

IN

SOUTHERN INDIA.

CHARGE OF THE HOOLIYA TUSKER.

SPORTING DAYS

IN

SOUTHERN INDIA:

BEING

REMINISCENCES OF TWENTY TRIPS IN PURSUIT OF BIG GAME, CHIEFLY IN THE MADRAS PRESIDENCY.

BY

LIEUT. COLONEL. A. J. O. POLLOCK,

Royal Scots Fusiliers.

WITH ILLUSTRATIONS.

LONDON:

HORACE COX,

WINDSOR HOUSE, BREAM'S BUILDINGS, E.C.

1894.

I DEDICATE THIS BOOK

TO MY SON

ANNESLEY,

IN THE HOPE THAT HE MAY BE SPARED TO ENJOY

AND BECOME PROFICIENT IN

ALL MANLY SPORTS OF THE FIELD,

THEREBY FULFILLING THE WISHES WHICH WERE

EXPRESSED BY HIS MOTHER A FEW

DAYS AFTER HIS BIRTH.

PREFACE.

In view of the numerous books on sport with big game which have been published, it requires a good deal of nerve to tackle such well-beaten ground; and although friends, on seeing the sketches in my shooting diaries, have repeatedly urged me to publish their contents, I have been very reluctant to do so.

A few months ago, however, it having become evident that a further spell of service in India was threatening me, I determined to follow their advice, and accordingly set to work on these rather hastily compiled pages, which were sent to the publishers in the month of June. The insertion of the half-page illustrations entailed some delay, as the letterpress could not be proceeded with until their precise positions and dimensions were fixed. The diaries which afforded me the necessary information were my companions during my jungle expeditions, and have suffered much from the wear and tear of camp life, more especially during the Monsoon trips, when many pages became obliterated by wet and exposure, or were lost owing to defective transport in the more remote jungles. Out of the mass of available material such portions only have been extracted as appeared to be interesting, but there is a good deal of sameness in big game shooting, and I am aware that my inferior powers of narration have failed to present the incidents dealt with in a sufficiently attractive form.

But few of the remarks on the habits of wild animals will be new to those who have visited the jungles—fewer still have been the result of my own discovery—the majority having been discussed either in the course of conversation, or in correspondence with acquaintances well skilled in jungle-lore, such as the late General Douglas Hamilton, Colonels Geoffrey Nightingale and Hooper, Major Frank Gordon-Cumming, Mr. Sanderson, and other celebrated hunters of big game, but—except where otherwise stated—they have been verified by personal experience, and the recipes have likewise been personally tested.

During the construction of the index it appeared that a rearrangement of a portion of the contents would be desirable, but my orders for embarkation being daily expected, no more time can be devoted to this work, nor can I even offer an excuse for its shortcomings, for—unlike others who have written on these subjects—it has been my misfortune during life to be obliged to wield the pen far oftener than the rifle.

My thanks are due to Mr. Charles Whymper and to Mr. Halls, the gentlemen who, from my crude water-colour sketches, have been able to evolve such artistic illustrations. My misleading brush must be entirely responsible for any inaccuracies which may become visible therein.

To Messrs. Walker and Boutall I am much indebted for reproducing the artists' pictures and my photographs so true to the originals.

ARTHUR POLLOCK.

22nd September, 1894.

CONTENTS.

CHAPTER I.

THE BEAR (*Ursus labiatus*).

CHAPTER II.

THE BEAR (*Ursus labiatus*).

CHAPTER III.

THE BEAR (*Ursus labiatus*).

CHAPTER IV.

THE PANTHER (*Felis pardus*).

CHAPTER V.

THE PANTHER (*Felis pardus*).

CHAPTER VI.

THE TIGER (*Felis tigris*).

CHAPTER IX.

THE INDIAN BISON (*Gavæus gaurus*).

CHAPTER X.

THE BISON (*Gavæus gaurus*).

CHAPTER XI.

THE ELEPHANT (*Elephas Indicus*).

CHAPTER XII.

THE ELEPHANT (*Elephas Indicus*).

CHAPTER XV.

MISCELLANEOUS.

CHAPTER XVI.

MISCELLANEOUS.

LIST OF ILLUSTRATIONS.

* Half-page illustrations.

PLEASURES OF A PIN-FIRE RIFLE.

CHAPTER I.

THE BEAR (*Ursus labiatus*).

Indian varieties of—Burmese bear—Sloth bears—Food of—Difficulty in aiming at correctly—Methods of shooting the—Beat at Poppinapett—Wounded bear charges—Nearly shot by a friend—Shoot first bear—Mad jackal—See a tiger—Bokur—Bears numerous at—Scouting for—Longevity of — The Tairbund Man-killers — Baliyah nearly caught—Absurd scene—Bears marked down—Am nearly scragged—Finale—Triumphal procession of villagers.

THREE varieties of bear are found in India, viz., the black and the brown bears of the Himalayas and Cashmere, and the black bear of the plains, inappropriately termed the sloth bear, for he is by far the most sporting animal of the lot.

Those who have pursued both varieties of the hill-bear declare that they afford but poor sport—the brown bear especially being a very timid animal—and never showing fight unless absolutely obliged to do so.

In this respect they both differ from the low-country animal, the majority of which are not only very plucky, but often distinctly aggressive.

There is also a variety found in Burmah—a diminutive edition of the black bear—which, owing to his size, affords no sport for the rifle, although a courageous little beast—he is known as a fruit bear.

The black bear* of the plains of India, the only member of the genus "Ursus" which I have as yet encountered, is about six feet long, and three feet high, but when standing on his hind legs—to which he is much addicted—his head would be about seven feet above the ground. He is a sufficiently formidable animal to give a spice of danger to his pursuit, while he at the same time lacks the dangerous aggressive powers of the tiger, or panther, and for this reason he is an excellent quarry to introduce the young sportsman to. One is inclined to take liberties with bears, that would not be attempted with the more dangerous kinds of big game; and, in consequence, many serious and fatal accidents have occurred. But, with ordinary steadiness, danger is reduced to a minimum.

He has a very keen nose, moderate sight, and ridiculous shambling gait; when galloping especially he is "all over the place." His long, shaggy hair shakes, and his limbs seem to be dislocated; but all the same, he

* *Ursus labiatus.*

gets over the ground much faster than a man can. A horse will soon overtake him on level ground, but dislikes close quarters with such an uncouth looking object.

He is nocturnal in his habits, leaving his fastnesses in the rocks about dusk, and, after passing the night foraging in the neighbouring country, returns thereto before sunrise.

Sometimes, when his rambles take him to distant feeding grounds, he does not get back till the sun is pretty high, and he not unfrequently lies up, in any shady spot he may find convenient, on the way home. In the hot weather the Mhowa* tree sheds its flowers, of which bears are particularly fond, and they then travel long distances, to any spot where these trees abound, lying up during the day in the vicinity. Nilghai and deer are also very partial to this flower, which smells abominably, but tastes sweet and luscious; and from which the natives distil a species of arrack, a strong spirit resembling rum. They are also very fond of white ants, whose habitations they destroy with their powerful claws, and then suck up the inmates, making a loud snoring noise while doing so.

In the Nizam's Dominions large groves—or topes—of the date palm, exist in many parts. The natives cut incisions in the stems of these trees, placing earthen vessels called "chatties" to catch the sap, which is sweet and pleasant to drink, and something like "Stone" ginger-beer, until it begins to ferment, which it rapidly does when the sun gets up. It then froths up like beer, and becomes sour, and intoxicating. Bears are very fond of this liquor, which is called toddy, and at night repair to

* Bassia.

the topes, smash the chatties, and lap up their contents to such an extent that they frequently become fuddled, and have difficulty in finding their way home.

I have only once seen bears in this state; but the toddy-wallahs—men who look after the topes—declare it is of common occurrence.

However, as a perfectly sober bear behaves in a peculiar way as a rule, and conducts himself irregularly, these statements must be received with reserve. The bear is also very fond of mangoes, sugar cane, wild figs, and many kinds of jungle fruits and roots; likewise grubs of sorts, to find which he upsets the stones under which they take refuge. So, wherever you find stones thus displaced, and ant-hills dug up, bears may be expected in the vicinity. With his excellent nose he discovers the nests of the large tree bee of India, and the trunks and branches will be found scored by his claws, in his endeavours to reach them; but, as these nests are generally suspended from light branches, at a good height from the ground, he can but seldom succeed; nor can he get at the nests of the rock bee, which are usually hung from an inaccessible ledge. The thick shaggy hide is quite proof against bee stings; but his nose is very tender, and in robbing the nests of ground bees he often gets severe punishment on this organ. The sportsman should give the nests of both rock and tree bees a wide berth; they are large and malignant insects, and will attack man or beast with slight provocation. On one occasion we were driven out of a camp under some mango trees, in which a colony of bees existed, the smoke from our camp fire bringing them down in dozens; but, luckily, it was after sunset, and we effected our retreat without much suffering, only two of the servants being stung.

In the Mysore and Annamullay jungles bears are reputed to eat the carcases of bison and elephants if they come across them. There is no doubt that tigers, panthers, and wild pigs do so, as I have frequently seen—or found the tracks of—these animals close by, and, judging from the habits of other members of the family, it is probable that our friend the black bear may also indulge in this way.* At one time, we used to consider the flesh of the bear quite a luxury; it tasted of roast beef with a dash of duck, and the hams used to be carefully put into brine and carried back to cantonments for the mess, when we were on short leave of absence. At Kowlass we shot a bear, and had some steaks cooked, which disagreed with us, in fact, we were all very unwell; and, after that experience, bears' meat disappeared from the menu.

The bear is often shot on returning from his night's wanderings, by lying in wait for him near his cave. The places resorted to by them always show unmistakable signs of their occupants; and all that is necessary is to be on the spot before daylight. It sometimes happens, in rocks near villages or roads, that the bear returns before daylight too, and he is met in the darkness near his own domains. This is unpleasant, for you cannot see the sights of your rifle well enough to aim properly, and a random shot may only wound, and make the animal dangerous. The outline of the brute is also very indistinct, and the proper spots to aim at cannot be seen; these are a dirty white horseshoe mark on the chest, and the usual place just behind the shoulder. In some positions you may brain him, or shoot him through the spine. When a bear charges, he will generally—not invariably—stand up on his hind legs when within a few yards, and all that is

* No authenticated proof exists on this point.

necessary is to aim just below the horseshoe and fire. When he charges right home on all fours, fire at his snout; it is white, and a good mark. The bullet then will either brain him or break his spine. In any case, you must hit him somewhere forward. You cannot miss at such a short range, and the impact of the bullet will check or turn him, giving a favourable opportunity for a decisive shot with the left barrel. It is not easy to place your bullet in the right spot, which is difficult to discern on his shaggy black coat, and you are very likely to "lose" your foresight, unless it is painted white. One dark morning, I came on two bears, close to their cave; the nearer one stood upon his hind legs, and began beating the air with his paws to frighten me. He was only fifteen yards off, but the lower part of his body was shrouded in darkness, and I could only just see his arms and head going through this pantomime against the faint light in the sky called the "crow's dawn." I fired and hit him, with the usual result, for, rushing on his comrade with shrieks of fury, he began to wool him, when, running forwards, I browned them with two more shots; they vanished into the darkness, and were never seen again; but the fighting and roaring continued at intervals till daylight, when we found they had entered an adjacent huge pile of rocks and baffled us. The most sporting way of shooting bears, is to bolt them from their stronghold with rockets and "kaweets," the fruit of the wood-apple, which is filled with powder and fitted with a fuse, the soft interior having been previously removed, leaving the hard outer shell, which thus becomes a hand grenade, and with lighted fuse is thrown into caves or fissures in the rock, where it bursts with a loud report. Panthers, and even tigers, sometimes appear on these occasions, and then the sport becomes more highly flavoured. This method is in every way preferable to the ambuscade system; it affords sport to all the party, and can be undertaken at any hour most convenient; moreover, the news of a kill seldom reaches camp before 9 a.m., and the early morning work is harassing, when followed by a long day's beating in the sun for a tiger that has killed. The off-days—those on which the tiger has not killed—are very tedious when passed in tents, and on such occasions we always went out for a casual beat, when a likely tract of jungle existed, remote from the tiger's haunts. My first encounter with a bear was in a jungle near Poppinapett, about fifty or sixty miles north of Secunderabad.

A brother officer was my companion. We were both tyros, and, having obtained a month's leave of absence, commenced operations by driving a rocky stretch of jungle, reputed to be the resort of bears. We started from camp on an elephant, which had been lent by H.H. the Nizam, and, having left it under a shady tree some distance off, took up our positions about half a mile ahead of the beaters, who, led by our shikaries, advanced in skirmishing order, making a tremendous din with tom-toms, horns, blank cartridge, and shouting. The caves in the rocks were searched by fireworks, and a bear was soon forced out, and headed straight for our position. We were posted on rocks, about three hundred yards apart, and on arriving within range, the bear was subjected to a heavy fire from both rifles, with the result that it was lamed, and could not travel fast over the rough ground. I was armed with a 12-bore pin-fire rifle, which, though by a maker of great repute, only burnt 2½ drachms of powder, and the cartridges after being fired almost invariably stuck in the breech. We both got down from our rocks, and kept up a running fire on the bear, which turned in my direction, and

I at length found myself within ten yards of it with both cartridges jammed, and the shikari with my second gun thirty yards behind me. At this juncture the bear turned round and charged. I bolted like a redshank, so did the shikari, who had the start of, and soon distanced me, but pulled up when he saw the brute gaining on me, and handed me the second gun. My friend now began firing to cover my retreat, His projectiles were whizzing all round, and it was difficult to aim steadily under the circumstances; but my two barrels stopped the bear, which again retired. The shikari now emerged from under a rock, and, pointing to a branch which had been broken by a bullet, said "it is better to be clawed by a bear than to eat the other sahib's bullets." We then followed the tracks up for some distance, and beat a hill for the brute, but never saw it again, so we returned disconsolately to camp. The elephant men declared that several bullets had passed close to them, and that one struck the howdah; and they pointed out a mark which might have been made by a ricochet. A few days later, at Nowsanpully, I got my first bear. Having started before daylight, and waited near a cave, two appeared, and, allowing them to approach within fifteen yards, I fired at the horseshoe of the leader, who turned round and savagely tackled his companion, expiring immediately afterwards. The second bear escaped.

The following morning I again went out, and saw no bears, but about seven o'clock a fine tiger stalked slowly across the plain towards the range on which I was posted; it was, however, headed by a wood-cutter, who commenced his work just at the wrong moment, and we failed to intercept it; this brute eventually became a notorious man-eater, of which more anon.

One day, in camp at Poppinapett, the village Patel (head man) came to ask us to shoot a mad jackal which had taken up his quarters in a rice field close by, and had bitten several natives, but on our way out we heard that an Arab had shot it with a match-lock. About twelve of the bitten natives came into camp and had their wounds cauterised, but six or seven succumbed to hydrophobia, as I afterwards heard, when in that district some years later, on a tiger shooting trip. During that expedition two friends (whom I will designate Poulton and Manley) of the 18th Hussars (who were then quartered at Secunderabad) and I, arrived at Bokur, some 150 miles to the north, early in April; the weather was very hot, and we had good fun with tigers, panthers, and bears, the last especially affording great sport. The surrounding country consisted for the most part of undulating ground, covered with long spear-grass, and dotted about with clumps of Palàs kino and custard apple bushes, with here and there a nullah shaded by thespesia, caroonda, and Indian beech trees. It was an unlikely looking jungle for bears, owing to the absence of caves and rocky ground, yet we met with a good many, which had evidently come from a distance, being attracted by the flowers of the Mhowa—a tree which was plentiful in that locality. Our plan of campaign was to repair in the early morning to some high ground near the camp, and there take up positions some distance apart, detaching local shikaries in pairs, to neighbouring points. These scouts had been ordered to follow and mark down any bears they might see; one of them was then to return with the news to the nearest sahib, or to the camp, the other remaining to watch the bear. The head shikari and his two assistants always visited the buffaloes that had been tied up for tigers in the early morning, and were back in camp before 10 a.m., and, in the absence of a *gāra* (kill), we could then proceed to tackle any bears that had been spotted by the scouts. We took it in turns to stalk the bear, the shooter being always accompanied by another sportsman in case of his help being required. Owing to the absence of good cover, the bears had often to lie down on very exposed spots, and their big black bodies could be easily seen from some distance. On arriving within twenty yards or so, the brute would generally wake up and "point" the shooter, who thereupon opened fire; sometimes it would charge at once on being awoke, but the result was nearly always the defeat and death of Bruin. It was not considered the correct thing to fire at him when asleep. The supporting rifle was very seldom called upon to fire, but the bear is a long-lived brute, unless the heart or brain are struck; and I remember at this place (Bokur) firing at a bear as he inspected me, not ten yards off, the bullet carried away the lower part of the brain-pan, but only seemed to daze him, and it was necessary to put a bullet through the neck, two through the shoulders, and one through the spine, before he gave up the ghost. The skull of this remarkably tough bear is still in my possession, together with several others, bearing similar traces of bullet wounds.

While here, news arrived one morning of a kill in a wooded glen at Tairbund, some four miles off. The villagers were particularly anxious that we should beat this place, in which two man-killing bears resided, from whence they used to make raids on the wood-cutters, with the result that two men and a woman had been killed, but not eaten, and several others severely bitten. We had tied up *haylas* (young buffaloes) there for tigers, therefore beating it had been deferred till a kill should be reported.

The head shikari, Baliyah, had sent some of his subordinates to collect beaters from the adjacent villages, and when we arrived at the glen, which was about a mile in length, and from 300 to 800 yards in breadth, he informed us that there were some tiger traces several days old, but that he thought the kill was by a *bōr butcha* (large panther). Accordingly we were posted in suitable trees near the centre of the valley, down which ran a shady nullah, having settled not to fire at anything but a tiger or panther during the first beat, and Baliyah ascended a small tree, about two hundred yards off, on our left front, to stop any animal attempting to break away in that direction.

The beaters were then sent word to commence. They were divided into parties by villages, each party being commanded by one of our shikaries, assisted by the *patel* of its particular village. They first started a panther, which failed to reach our line, and shortly afterwards the two famous man-killing bears were afoot, and attempted to break out at Baliyah's tree, which was a stunted and weak one, and would not bear him higher than twelve feet or so. Throwing a stick, he commenced shouting at them, to cause them to turn down the hill towards us, but, so far from having the desired effect, one of the bears coolly commenced to climb up to scrag him; however, the tree was too light, and, although within a yard, he could not quite reach him. Baliyah was at the end of a branch which threatened to break every moment, and his execrations of the bear were mingled with piteous appeals to us to come to his assistance, but he was too far off, and we were laughing so much, it was impossible to aim correctly. At length the bears, ceasing their efforts to reach him, made off across the top of the valley to a small ravine half a mile away, where they were duly marked down. The beaters soon arrived at our alignment; some of them bore traces of former encounters with these very bears; they were woodcutters, and stated that, when engaged at their occupation, they had been attacked by these brutes without any provocation; two had been terribly bitten and clawed about the face and arms,* others had escaped by climbing trees, or running away, and—as has been already stated—several had succumbed to their injuries.

The ravine in which the bears had been marked down, lay between two small, stony hills, studded with a few straggling trees, devoid of foliage. These hills afforded no cover, but the ravine contained some large boulders. It joined the valley we had just left, some three hundred yards further down. We were posted on the opposite bank, and the beaters commenced to work from the top of the nearer hill, taking the nullah cross-wise. The bears showed at once, and tried to charge back through the line of beaters, but were received with volleys of blank cartridge and rockets, and such a terrific din, that they were gradually forced forward in our direction. Again and again did they try to break back, but in vain. The beaters worked splendidly; their blood was up, and they were determined to vanquish their foes, which were gradually pushed back across the ravine on to the line of guns, passing me about sixty yards off, heading towards Poulton, who was on my right. He left his post, and came nearer to me to intercept the bears, which he thought might have passed midway between us, at rather a long shot distant from either post,

* The poor wretches had had their arms nearly bitten off above the elbow, and although the limbs had knitted in a marvellous manner, they were quite useless.

DEATH OF THE TAIRBUND MAN-KILLERS.

but the brutes saw him moving, and headed straight up to me. One was slightly larger than the other, and I took it first, but although the bullet hit there was no effect apparent beyond the usual woolling of its comrade, which returned the compliment very spiritedly, and a rough-and-tumble fight ensued. This was followed by a shot from Poulton, who was some distance off, and a right and left from me, which led to further furious onslaughts between the brutes, during which I distributed my leaden favours with great impartiality into the middle of the struggling mass, now within thirty yards. At last the big bear discerned the common enemy, and galloping up to within a few yards, rose on her hind legs and advanced with outstretched arms to embrace me, at a moment when a cartridge case in my pin-fire rifle became jammed in the loader's hands, but I had just time to insert one cartridge and fire at the horse-shoe, the muzzle almost touching her chest, a fleeting hope passing through my mind that she would not knock it aside with her paws. Over she rolled —not quite dead, but, as I afterwards found, shot through the lungs. To strike the heart aim should be taken *under* the horse-shoe mark when the bear is in this position. During this scrimmage the natives had shouted out "the bears have killed the sahib" (meaning me), and Poulton and Manley now arrived breathless, and we polished off the second bear without difficulty, it being badly wounded and hardly able to walk.

The villagers were in great delight. A triumphal procession was formed; the bears were tied on a cart and taken to camp, headed by a band of horns and tom-toms, and surrounded by a large crowd singing and dancing. They did not arrive till nearly midnight, having been exhibited at all villages near the homeward route.

Up to this time we had had some difficulty in obtaining a sufficient number of beaters from the neighbouring villages, although we took it in turns to see every man paid daily on production of a wad, with which they were individually served out in the morning, but the destruction of these bears so increased our popularity that the camp was daily invaded by far more men than we required during the remainder of our time at Bokur.

CHAPTER II.

THE BEAR (*Ursus labiatus*).

The big bear of Burbose—Is shot by Poulton—Bear at Loashera—Spearing tournament—The bear is victorious—Shoot she-bear and capture cub—Cub routs our visitors—Murrel fishing—March to Mowtool—Affair with bear—Bear spearing by Colonel Nightingale—Dislike of horses to—Jamakapett—Bears' Paradise—Shoot three bears—Expenditure of ammunition—A warm corner—Kill three more bears—Capture cub—Pugnacity of bears—Peculiar bone—Its properties—Bears reputed to kidnap women—Bear spear.

THE bears of the Central Provinces, in the Madras Presidency, have the reputation of being the largest and most ferocious in Southern India.

Although they never eat the bodies of their victims, they annually kill a considerable number of natives—chiefly wood-cutters, who make their livelihood by gathering fuel in the jungles inhabited by these animals.

The largest black bear I ever saw was shot at a place named Burbose, in the Koobair district, Nizam's Dominions, where we arrived on the 17th April, 1871. About 2 P.M. a scout brought in news of a bear, so we sallied forth, but meanwhile the brute had changed his quarters, and we saw him ascend a steep hill covered with long grass, about a mile away. Poulton and Manley went up the hill and I guarded the base. After two hours' patrolling the bear broke on the opposite side of the hill from me, but was marked into a nullah, headed back by a village shikari, and finally despatched by Poulton, who put a bullet through his heart as he was crossing him, at a range of about eighty yards. We held a *post mortem* on him and found twenty-one lobes on his liver, and as the natives say that each lobe means a year, this was a regular veteran, a fine male bear about 6 feet 8 inches long.

At Loashera in the Neermul district, we had great fun with a bear one morning. It was Manley's turn to fire, I being in support, and the brute was taking his siesta in the cleft of a huge rock, under the shade of a kino tree. We stalked up quietly to within twenty yards, when he suddenly got up and peered out at us; his white snout caught my eye, but Manley could not see him, nor would he let me fire. The result was, that the bear retired further into the cleft, and, bolting from the far side, was 150 yards away before we again sighted him, as he lobbed across some open ground towards an isolated cluster of rocks half a mile off. We both fired, and one shot lamed him slightly, but on he went. Our horses and spears were not far away, so we shouted for them, and then ran after the bear as hard as we could. Knowing he was steering for the cairn, we took a short cut, and he was not very far ahead of us when he reached it and rushed in. This was followed by a great turmoil inside, guttural growls, and roars, and shrieks of the bear, and it was evident that a rough and tumble fight was going on with some savage occupant who was in previous possession. We had by this time arrived close to the rocks, the subterranean conflict suddenly ceased, and out dashed a large panther, which, bounding over some rocks, caught sight of Manley, and crouched close to him, watching him as a cat does a mouse. At first it appeared to be a tiger, about to spring on Manley, who was quite unconscious of his danger, so I

BRUIN TRIUMPHANT.

shouted "Look out, there is a tiger just over your head," and, keeping my sights on the brute, told Manley to move to the left, as of course it would be dangerous to fire until he was well clear of the jānwar. A few seconds after the panther retired up a sloping sheet of rock towards the cairn, and I fired a shot, the ricochet of which struck him in the ball of the off fore paw, as we afterwards discovered. On re-entering the cairn there was another huge scuffle inside, followed by the exit of the bear, which headed across an open plain, towards a range of hills rather over a mile from us.

My horse had not arrived, but Poulton, who had just ridden up, and Manley, whose syce was fleeter of foot than mine, took their spears and pursued the bear. So I climbed up the cairn and witnessed a most amusing scene. The bear, being rather lame, was soon overtaken, Poulton leading, and doing all he knew to get the spear, closely pressed by Manley. The plain was studded with stunted acacias, kino, and custard apple bushes, and a good many anthills—not bad going on the whole, but trappy. Poulton soon arrived within spear's length, and was in the act of delivering his thrust, when the bear turning sharply round, charged him with roars of anger His horse swerved off, and Manley's pony, close behind, turned round and made a clean bolt of it, but soon put its foot in a hole, and came down—no harm done, so Manley mounted again, Poulton, in the meanwhile, tackling the bear, but with like result, his horse Pyjamas again stampeding. For fully twenty minutes this absurd performance continued, the bear steadily gaining ground towards the hills, at the foot of which was a tank with a large bund (embankment) covered with date palms; this he eventually reached, after a final engagement with his tormentors, who were again worsted and routed ignominiously.

I then despatched a cooly to ask them to return to tackle the panther,* but Poulton had met with some antelope, and was stalking them. Manley, however, arrived after an hour, and the afternoon's proceedings are detailed in the chapter devoted to panthers.

The following morning Poulton and I went out early to look for bears, in a small rocky hill about four miles from camp.

We found on arrival that there was only room for one rifle, so we tossed up for first shot, which Poulton won. In a short time a bear suddenly appeared within twenty yards. Poulton fired and rolled her over, whereupon a young one, which we had not hitherto seen, jumped off her back, and commenced running round in a circle, giving vent to the most heartrending shrieks. The old bear rose again, but speedily got a quietus. A most exciting chase then commenced after the cub, which would not let anybody go near him; the little beggar charged us furiously, and at first we bolted, although he was not much larger than a spaniel.

At length we found that the best way to collar him was to let him charge close up to our legs, then stooping down, to lift him smartly into the air, by the hair of his back, so that he could not bite—thus, with the aid of a cumbley (blanket), we secured and took him to camp, where a small cage was made for his residence.

We were encamped near the village, in a mango tope, of which some of the trees bore very good fruit—not the turpentiney abominations generally found in the jungle,

* The shikaries had discovered him in an adjacent cave while the bear tournament was in progress.

but real graft mangoes—and Baliyah, who, in addition to being head shikari, made himself generally useful in camp, volunteered to climb up to get some for us. In the course of his operations, however, he disturbed a nest of the red tree ant, the occupants of which vigorously attacked him. He shouted with pain, and declaring he was being eaten alive, came down like a flash of lightning, barking the skin of his legs in his rapid descent. On reaching the ground he rolled over and over to get rid of his persecutors, which bit so severely that their heads remained embedded in his skin after the bodies had been rubbed off. Later on in the day, some of the local native magnates visited the camp to see our trophies. In the middle of the function the young bear was enlarged, and immediately charged the gaily attired groups of grandees, and their retainers. A complete rout ensued, all dignity being sacrified, in a stampede for the village; it was ridiculous to see the tiny brute, chasing a crowd of twenty men, who flew along with shouts of alarm, and turbans wildly streaming in the air. He managed to bite two of them, and we ourselves had a pretty lively time before we got him into his cage again—but we were not again troubled by visitors. From a small and nearly dried-up tank, close to the camp, we got several good hauls of murrell, with nets, several of the fish being about three pounds weight, and not in the least muddy in taste—a nice change from everlasting "ishtoo" (stew) and curry.

Some days after this we arrived at Mowtool, and news was brought in of a bear and a dooker (pig) said to be lying under some shady bushes, within a short distance of each other, so we rode out in hopes of being able to use the spear, but a glance at the ground showed this to be impossible. It was Manley's turn to fire—I being in support—and Poulton was detached to the off side of the valley, wherein the jānwars were reclining, but before we began our stalk the bear got his wind, and came slowly up the hill towards us. Directly Manley caught sight of him he fired an ineffective snap-shot, and the bear, dashing through the scrub jungle, some forty yards off, charged a squad of beaters towards our left rear. I gave him two barrels, and turned him with the second—the bullet, striking his forepaw, inflicted a trifling wound. He then recrossed the valley towards Poulton, whose rifle we soon heard, and shortly afterwards, seeing the bear heading back for a range of hills in our rear, I mounted and pursued him, but could not get within spearing distance, owing to the rocky nature of the ground. He gained the hill, and was finally marked down into a nullah, thickly fringed with kino, jāmun, and Indian beech; here we came upon him later in the day, and, after a spirited encounter, finished him—a very fine male bear.

It will be evident, from these stories, that a great deal of lead was frequently expended on bears without much apparent result, the fact being that unless the brain, spine, or heart are hit, bullets have little or no effect, indeed, merely act as stimulants.

Before approaching a bear that appears to be dead, load both barrels, and be ready for instant action; they have an awkward trick of shamming dead, and when you come within range, may make a desperate attempt to embrace you—a bear *in articulo mortis* becomes quite revivified if he catches your eye, and we had some narrow escapes in consequence before we discovered this peculiarity. The exploits of the late Colonel Nightingale with rifle and spear were well known in the Deccan—and about bear spearing, in particular, there were many anecdotes associated with his name—he, having discovered certain haunts of bears situated in rideable country, used to go out alone from Secunderabad, and have excellent sport with the spear.

In spite of the disasters of the Loashera day, we were always on the look out for a chance of retrieving our reputations, and such chances did from time to time occur, but of so fleeting a nature that we could never take advantage of them, for, like opportunities for effective action of cavalry, they were transient, and the two gallant hussars who were with me never afterwards got an opening for attack.

Horses, as a rule, loathe bears, and one which will enter with zest into pursuit of panther or pig, will often decline a close interview with Bruin; nor is this to be wondered at, they are such ugly and ungainly looking brutes when galloping, and give vent to such unearthly shrieks—often accompanied by hostile demonstrations with the paws on the approach of the spearman—that it requires a more than ordinarily phlegmatic or courageous horse to face them—their smell, too, is very repugnant to horses as well as elephants.

My horse, a chesnut waler, an old pig-sticker, whose legs bore many honourable scars of boars' tusks, would, after sniffing the body of a dead tiger, step quietly over it, but he always jumped over the body of a bear, declining to smell it. Our shikaris assured us that at a place named Jamakapett we should have ample opportunities of spearing bears; and after sundry adventures with tigers and other animals, we duly arrived there in the middle of May. We encamped in a mango tope, near a large tank, and found the surrounding country a regular bear's paradise.

Mango topes, send-bunds, sugar cane khets (fields), and groves of Mhowa trees were in great profusion, and large tracts of scrub jungle, studded with isolated hills, and some piles of rocks, afforded cool and shady retreats during the day, and had evidently been patronised by bears for many years, large mango trees forcing their way up through clefts in the rocks from the ursine deposits below.

But, so far as spearing bears was concerned, we were doomed to disappointment, the particular zone of jungle where this was to have been done being deserted by them. The shikari pointed out the maidan, where Nightingale and Hebbert (Horse Artillery) had had several successful mornings' sport with bears returning from their nocturnal rambles—but none appeared to us, nor were there any fresh traces in the hills environing this open ground. He (Baliyah) also spent several hours searching for a watch which Hebbert Sahib had lost some years before when riding a bear, but he failed to find it.

We had, however, some capital sport with the rifle in other parts of the neighbouring country. The first day we went out in the morning, and two bears fell to my rifle, right and left, but without any circumstances of interest: my friends saw no jānwars of any kind, although the shikaris declared that the place was full of bears.

After tiffin we went out for a casual beat to a cairn about four miles off, where a bear was soon dislodged, but took refuge in another pile of boulders, where for two hours we assailed him with fireworks before he could be induced to bolt. He then headed across an open plain, towards a hill about half a mile off, and a vast expenditure of ammunition took place at long ranges, which resulted in his falling, pierced by many bullets, far out in the maidan. He was a very fine male bear, with a sleek and handsome skin, quite different to the ordinary kind.

There was no news of tigers, so next day after tiffin we started on the elephant for the same ground. On the way we came to a small hill, crowned by a heap of boulders, which projected down the slope on one side till it reached a neck or coll, some fifty yards long, which connected it with another and smaller hill covered with scrub jungle and detached rocks. We were posted on the neck at the start, but in the stress of the action that followed, the two guns on my left gradually moved farther back and to their left. It was an insignificant looking spot, and we had passed it by the previous afternoon, not considering it worth beating. The beaters advanced from the far side of the hill in our front, and on arriving at the rocks plied them with fireworks, soon forcing out a bear, which came straight down the hill and thence along the coll, passing within twenty yards of me—on the left—but I could not fire, as he was heading straight for Poulton's post, which commanded mine. I heard him fire three shots, and then Manley on the extreme left opened fire; but, being unable to move from the rock I was posted on, without running the chance of stopping a stray bullet, all that was going on in that direction was unseen by me. Immediately the firing ceased another bear descended by the same path as his predecessor, but inclined slightly to the right and halted. My shot struck him somewhere, and he then took the same line as the first bear, down to Poulton—whom I momentarily expected to fire; but it subsequently transpired that he had left his ground in order to examine the body of the first bear, which, having been wounded by him, went on towards Manley, and was killed there.

The shikaries, from the top of the cairn, now shouted that the brute was escaping, and on turning round I saw him some eighty yards off, crossing the smaller hill behind me. The first shot, striking low, missed him, but a shell from the left barrel went through the shoulder, and he fell dead in his tracks without a groan. Turning round, I had barely reloaded when another bear moved up the hill, and then turned to the right straight along the line of beaters, which receded as he approached. I gave him a shell when he was about seventy yards off, which rolled him over, but he got up again, and, charging right through the beaters, vanished over the top of the hill. I then went to see what had become of Poulton, and met him returning to his post after examining the dead bear, and, as there was only room for one rifle on the coll, I elected to remain spectator for the rest of the beat. In a short time another bear appeared, moving across our left front towards Manley, who got a long shot at but missed him. It had the effect, however, of checking the brute, which turned and attempted to break back through the beaters. Poulton called me down to help, and some shells fired by us, which burst on the rocks near him, caused him to change his mind, and he turned again and passed straight under Manley, who was again unlucky. Poulton ran on to cut off his retreat, and I remained smoking on the rock. Poulton fired twice, but failed to stop him. He then shouted to me to run up the hill in rear, which I did, directed by the elephant men from the lower ground, who could see all the entertainment, but on reaching the crest it was only to see the bear lobbing across the plain over two hundred yards away, and both my shots missed him, although the shell from the left barrel burst close to him, and made him swerve off with a roar of disapproval. He, however, made good his retreat to a tangle of acacia among some rocks half a mile off.

We then returned to track up the wounded bear, which, after breaking through the line of beaters, had made his way across some open ground to the scene of operations of the preceding afternoon. We tracked him into the cave by his blood. He was very hard hit, and we could hear him close by, evidently dying, when suddenly the beaters outside began to shout "Reech ăta" (a bear is coming), and on emerging we saw a large bear, followed by a cub, advancing across the plain at a gallop towards the rocks we were on. Whenever the old bear got too far ahead the little chap began to screech, and the big one would immediately stop and wait for it. They came straight to the foot of the rocks, but winded us, and went off again, pursued by Manley, who caught the youngster, but it was suffocated shortly after by the coolies, who feared its cries would recall its mother. The cave was explored by the shikaries, who found my wounded bear had died, and the body was brought out without difficulty.

The bullet had passed through the lungs. Sometimes, when stalking, we used to come suddenly on bears grubbing for roots, &c. In such cases the chances are that the brute will charge without further provocation. A boar behaves in the same way, and it sometimes became necessary to fire in self-protection, even at the risk of disturbing nobler game. The fat of the bear is useful for rheumatic pains, if well rubbed in, but falls short of tiger's fat in efficacy. The male bear possesses a peculiar bone, similar to that of the otter, which natives of both sexes prize highly as a remedy for sterility. These bones are in great demand,

and disappear as rapidly as the beernecks and fat of a tiger. Consequently the Sahib must take charge of this talisman if he wishes to secure one.

In the Deccan—and, indeed, all over Southern India—a widespread belief prevails among natives of all creeds and classes, that the male bear is in the habit of carrying off native women to the jungle. The shikaries often declare that some of their own friends have been thus treated, and they will mention the names of the ladies and the localities they disappeared from. One of my shikaries (Baliyah) informed me that he knew a woman who returned after being absent for three years in the jungles in this way, and that a young girl who had been spirited away mysteriously for several months, one day found her way back to her village, and accounted for her absence by a similar story.

Both women stated that they had met with very kind treatment, but that the food was bad. All natives to whom I have spoken on this subject are evidently firmly convinced that such cases do occur, but if any incredulity is evinced. they cease their revelations forthwith.

On asking Baliyah how he accounted for the Tairbund bears having attacked some women and killed others, he immediately replied that they must be female bears, and were therefore jealous, for no male would either bite or claw a woman. Strange to say, his theory was afterwards proved to be true, and he took special care to point this out to me on the death of the bears a week later on.

One of the shikaries should always carry a bear-spear, a weapon which not unfrequently renders good service. The head should be three inches broad and six long, and it must be welded to a long iron socket to protect the shaft, which should be of wood, not bamboo, for one foot of its length; it must also be fitted with a cross-bar, about eighteen inches from the spear point, to prevent it from jamming in an animal, and to stop him from wriggling along it and seizing the spearman.

CHAPTER III.

THE BEAR (*Ursus labiatus*).

A long-lived bear—Elephant's game of football—Rajumpett—Bāban Sahib the sorcerer—Bear marked down—Bāban's behaviour—Shoot the bear—Cholera—Ulleepoor—Former experiences there—The Ulleepoor man-eater—His death—Bears near Singareny—My colonel kills two and wounds a third—Bears at Penconda—Shoot two—Effect of Express bullet—Bears at Mulkapoor—Bears in Mysore—Bout with Bandipore bears—Wounded bear dies—Antics of wounded bears — Inebriated bears — Fatal accident with bear — Hybernating — Cold weather shooting trips — Wounds inflicted by bears.

The bears in the Jamakapett district, although affording good sport, lacked the pugnacity of those met with in the Godavery country further north. The natives also gave them a very good character, and stated that they were seldom molested, unless they met them face to face in the jungle, under which circumstances the most peaceably disposed bear becomes aggressive, being stimulated by the instinct of self-preservation.

A few days after the final events of the last chapter, we went out to have another beat for bears at the warm corner, and found one "at home," which forthwith charged up the hill through the beaters—luckily without doing any harm—and, crossing some open ground, was marked into a ravine, on a jungle-covered ridge at the opposite side. We finished the beat, and followed him; but in the meanwhile he had shifted his ground, and entered the cairn before described. I was posted on the extreme right, facing the hill as a long stop, my friends being closer to the cairn, and, believing that due warning would be given by their rifles of any jānwar coming in my direction, I was taking it easy, and smoking a pipe under a shady tree.

During the beat something moving among the bushes on the right caught my eye, and presently a bear emerging therefrom, passed me about sixty yards off, at the other side of a rocky nullah. On getting my right barrel, he turned round and bit his hind leg savagely; then, catching sight of me, he charged, receiving my fire until he collapsed under a bush close by. Meanwhile, hearing Poulton shout, I was obliged to watch the progress of the beat, and, on turning round again, there was the bear fifty yards off, and going gaily away! Two more shots stopped him for ever, and, on examination, we found he had been hit by two bullets in the head, one through the near shoulder, two just behind the heart, and the first shot had struck him in the thigh. One of those in the head must have grazed the brain and temporarily stunned him. He had passed close to my friends, but had been hidden by the rough ground. The elephant men asked that the elephant might be allowed to play with the carcase, which was carried down and placed before him. An amusing game of football then took place, the elephant shuffling the body between his fore and hind legs for some seconds, then projected it backwards with the fore legs, and took a flying shot at it with one of the ponderous hind legs, which invariably missed the mark. At length he made a "bull's-eye," and sent the carcase spinning away for ten yards. Then he became so excited he charged us, and we dare not approach him for nearly an hour. He was a vindictive brute, and had killed five of his mahouts.

A week later, at Rajumpett, a village shikari, rejoicing in the name of Baban Sahib, was introduced to us. A ferocious-looking desperado—beard dyed red with henna, blue turban and tunic, and a leather shikar belt covered with muntars (charms) and daggers. He had an evil reputation as a sorcerer (jādū wallah), and the shikaries were awed by him.

Late in the afternoon he sent coolies in to camp, to say he had a bear marked down for us. It was my turn to shoot; so I went out on the elephant to the trysting place, where Baban was waiting, armed with a percussion musket, and full of swagger. As we approached the spot where the bear was lying, he halted the other shikaries, and led me for a short distance up a small hill, on which a few trees were studded at intervals. He now exhibited signs of reluctance to advance, and his swagger vanished. After a few minutes we arrived at the foot of a steep slope, about forty yards long, on the top of which was a big rock indented by a deep fissure, in which a creeper was growing, covered with thick foliage, which obscured the interior. When within ten yards the bear, standing on his hind legs, peered out through the leaves. This was too much for Baban, who turned about and made a clean bolt of it. My shot struck the bear in the neck, and he collapsed on the spot. Baliyah witnessed Baban's defeat, and was intensely amused, declaring he was an impostor, and the jādū (magic) a fraud. We then marched for several days, through a cholera-stricken country, having great difficulty in obtaining bēgāris to show us the jungle tracks, eventually arriving at Ulleepoor, a beautiful spot, surrounded by hills and lochs, like the Highlands of

Scotland. I had been here once before, during a shooting trip in the monsoon, when the heavy rains being too much for a bechoba (without pole) tent, recourse was had—with the approval of the head man of the village—to a Mahommedan mosque for shelter. Here, however, a swarm of bees, which was located in certain "properties" in a loft, being roused by the smoke, drove both me and my followers back to the jungle. Our present camping ground was near a pretty tank, a grassy sward intervening, and tree jungle stretching away on every side.

Some years previously, this had been the haunt of a notorious man-eating tiger, in pursuit of which a party of sahibs arrived one morning, and pitched their camp under the very trees we had selected for ours. While they were at breakfast some brinjarries came running in to report, that one of their number had just been carried off by a tiger. One of them, a doctor sahib, took his rifle, ran across to the spot indicated by the natives, and, attired in pyjamas and slippers, entered the jungle, where he found the brute on the body of its victim, and brained it first shot. In the hot weather of 1881 my colonel and I had a good morning's sport with bears near Rajavole, in the Singareny district. The weather had been intensely hot, and when Kistiah* reported no gāra, the days passed very slowly indeed. Accordingly, inquiries were made if any part of the jungle infested by bears could be beaten without disturbing the tiger ground, and the head shikari reported that such ground did exist near a certain hill some four miles east of the camp. The following morning, reports of no gāra having again arrived, we sent on forty coolies and rode out after breakfast to try for the bears. The ground consisted of a rocky ridge 150 yards long, terminating in a

* Our head shikari.

heap of large boulders and "perched blocks," that curious formation of the Hyderabad country. The bears' caves were situated at this end; the surrounding jungle consisted of straggling and stunted trees, with occasional rocks. The grass had been burned at the beginning of the hot weather in the usual way, to ensure a growth in the monsoon. Not a green bush of any sort was visible, and it was a desolate and dreary-looking wilderness. The colonel was posted on the top of the ridge at the end remote from the rocks, I being at the foot and to the left front. The beat having commenced from the rocky end, some jānwars were started, which I could not see; but presently the colonel fired four shots, and the beaters began to recoil—clear proof that a beast of some sort was heading towards them. Kistiah now came running down to say "the colonel has killed two bears and wounded a third, which has gone back into a cave—come and shoot it." So, sending word to the colonel, off I went. To reach the entrance of the cave, it was necessary to slide down some steep rocks, but a few yards further on, the way was blocked by a large boulder, which formed a sort of platform, shoulder high. The bear was here, and within six feet; but, owing to the darkness, it was impossible to see either him or the rifle sights. In a minute or so my eyes got more accustomed to the gloom, and his snout was dimly to be seen; not so the foresight. However, by raising and lowering the muzzle, which alternately obscured and disclosed his snout, sufficient aim was obtained to send a bullet through his brain. One is not so brave when tigers are concerned! We dragged him out, and found that the colonel's bullet had hit him in the ball of a hind foot as he was galloping away. The beat had not lasted half an hour, and we were back in camp in time for tiffin. During this expedition we were joined by

Colonel J. C. Russell (12th Lancers), and as our time was short, and we had a lot of ground before us, we were pushing on for the Pakhāl Lake, only stopping for a day or two at the most likely places on the way. At Mankote we had a kill by a bōr butcha, and on our march to Penconda had a beat for him. He did not show, but during the beat, preceded by swarms of peafowl, a bear passed near me, going straight for Colonel Russell, and I soon heard both my companions open fire. At the end of the beat we found the bear lying dead within a short distance of their posts. He had run the gauntlet of both their rifles. We then had another beat, during which a bear charged out to me. The right barrel rolled him over, as we thought, dead; but, after a few seconds, up he got and bolted between me and the Colonel, who hit him hard, causing him to jump clean off the ground into the air; nevertheless, he gained the shelter of the hill we had first beaten, closely followed by Kistiah and me. Here he entered a cave and was attacked by my Colonel and Kistiah, Colonel Russell and I taking refuge from the heat and glare in a little grotto at the foot of the hill.

Here we had been coffee-housing for some time, and expatiating on the glories of shooting in the Highlands, when suddenly two shots on the top of the hill put us on the *qui vive*, and we just had time to clear out, when down came the bear to the very spot; but we had no difficulty in shooting him, as he stood facing us a short distance off. My first shot had entered his back, just over the point of the near shoulder, and opening out on the ribs, had made an ugly but harmless wound—this was with a ·500 Express, the bullet of which is, I think, generally too light. Good sport with bears was also obtainable near Mulkapoor and Markudpully, on the Masulipatam road, and in the country towards Toomulgooduim; but these districts were reserved for operations in the cold weather, on account of the good small-game shooting they then also afforded, and of their suitability for short leave of absence. The cream of the bear country in that part of India lies thirty miles on each side of a line joining Secunderabad and Chandah, and during one trip we met no less than forty-five bears, in part of that zone, although much of our time was then devoted to tigers. They are also fairly plentiful in Mysore; but, as a rule, the thick jungles there, and in the Shimoga, Billiga, Rungum, and Annamullay forests, are unfavourable for good sport with any jānwars, except bison or elephants, which, owing to their size, cannot easily conceal themselves.

One morning in December, 1881, at Bandipore, near Gopaulswamy Hill, when searching for a rogue elephant, I struck the fresh trail of two bears, which were followed up without difficulty, through the long green grass and creepers, to a wooded slope, dotted with glades, in which the grass was quite six feet high. My battery consisted of a double-barrel 10-bore rifle, burning seven drachms of powder, and a ·500 Express, the latter being carried by Busma, a local shikari. After a mile we entered a dense patch of spear grass, surrounding some large rocks. The traces were very fresh here, and on turning the corner of a rock, I came face to face with a large bear not five yards off. He had heard us coming, and was standing up on his hind legs, his head and neck only showing above the high grass, ears cocked and eyes sparkling, evidently resenting intrusion, and about to become aggressive. The head and shoulders of his spouse appeared alongside him; she had been grubbing up some roots, and had just realised the situation. The rascal Busma now bolted with the Express,

A WELCOME TO BANDIPORE.

although he had been very steady in an engagement with bison some days previous. No time was to be lost, so I fired the 10-bore in the bear's face, and down he went, giving me an opportunity as he lay on the ground of using the left barrel, which most provokingly missed fire, owing to a bad cap in the cartridge.

The usual scene then occurred; he got up and went for his companion, and the forest resounded with shrieks and roars. I reloaded, but it was difficult to get a good opening at my friends, owing to the long grass; however, I browned the struggling mass, and soon fired away the four cartridges in my possession, the remainder being with the errant Busma, who, after much objurgation, mingled with entreaty, brought up the Express. In the meanwhile the bears had been slowly descending the hill—fighting every twenty yards, both being wounded and irascible—and each looking upon its companion as the cause of its misfortunes. Busma was no longer worthy of confidence, so with a rifle over each shoulder I advanced to the attack. The bears were now sixty yards down the hill, fighting in some long grass, whence the usual uproar emanated, as I half ran, half slid, down the slope; but, by the time the spot was reached the music was reduced to a solo, one of the combatants having bolted after severely mauling its companion, who remained rolling about on the ground giving vent to demoniacal howls. I made a bad shot with the Express, hitting it low down in a fore paw, and it went off at a fine pace on the remaining three legs. Believing it was my original antagonist I followed, but the marks of blood were but slight, and ceased altogether at the end of half a mile, so I retraced my steps and soon hit off the other trail, which gave ample evidence of a severe wound. The gunbearer having meanwhile come up and taken the second rifle, we followed the track to within a mile of the Tippicado road, and then desisted, as it was past mid-day—we had not breakfasted—and the bungalow was six miles off. Next day news arrived that the bear had been found dead near a police station on the road, close to where we left off the pursuit, and that, in addition to a wound in the neck, it had been hit twice in the body. Even when in full view of its real enemy it is very odd how a bear will always go for its companion. I remember on one occasion two friends were out with me and we were beating a steep slope, covered with thick jungle, into which three bears had been marked. The beaters began at the bottom of the hill to beat up towards us, our movements being controlled by the head shikari from the opposite plateau, who signalled which way the bears were going, the jungle being too thick for us to see them till they emerged on the open ground at the top, which they did within ten yards of us. Each man took his bear and fired; they all rolled over wounded but got up again, whereupon the two flank bears with one accord attacked the centre one ferociously, and the huge mass began to roll down the hill under the close fire of our rifles. We were within a few yards of them in open ground, and they could not have helped seeing us.

It is very amusing to watch a party of bears returning from their forays in the early morning; they are often as full of fun as monkeys, and it is hard to fire at them after enjoying a view of their uncouth but amusing gambols. As with human beings, there is generally one member of the party who is a butt for the others, and who is consequently subjected to a lot of rough usage. I remember one morning seeing three bears coming across a maidan towards a rocky hill on which I was posted close to their fastnesses. They behaved in such a ridiculous manner that there was no doubt in my mind that they were the worse for drink, rolling about from side to side when on their hind legs, pushing each other over and fighting at intervals. This was in a district that contained many send-bunds, the owners of which complained that they sustained great loss by the nightly visits of the bears to their chatties, which they invariably broke in order to lap up the contents. As they neared my post the leading bear was about thirty yards ahead of his companions, coming straight up a rocky track towards me; he stopped for a few seconds to turn over a stone in search of grubs, and I stepped into the middle of the path while he was thus engaged, and remained perfectly steady; he resumed his advance without noticing me, so I coughed slightly to attract his attention; for some seconds he was dumb-foundered and could hardly believe his eyes. Then, standing up on his hind legs, he made hostile demonstrations with his paws in the air to frighten me, and then turned viciously on a small tree at the edge of the track and tore branches off it evidently with the same object. A shot through the horseshoe immediately afterwards finished him. Poor brute, I often regret having fired that shot. His companions bolted and were not again seen. It is inadvisable to fire at a bear or any other dangerous animal straight above you on higher ground; this is the only shot that is barred in bear shooting. At the same time a certain amount of respect is due to a bear; his offensive powers are underrated, and many serious and even fatal accidents have occurred thereby, the last I remember being that of the death of the plucky young Lord Edward St. Maur, who was so severely bitten by a wounded bear which he had followed up, that he succumbed to the effects of amputation a few days afterwards.

The bear of the plains of India is the only animal of his tribe that does not hybernate. There is no reason for his doing so, for his food is obtainable throughout the year, so he is always available for sport. When the cold weather sets in, and the small game shooting trips are organised about Christmas, his pursuit often proves an agreeable change from that of the everlasting snipe and duck. Moreovcr these parties frequently include members who go out merely for picnicking and not from anxiety to slay small game. A bear, however, is sufficient to put them on their mettle, and to make them keener for sport; and it often happens that the uncertainties of the chase bring the brunt of the encounter on them.

There is no sport so fertile in ridiculous incidents as bear shooting, chiefly owing to the eccentric nature of the brute himself; but these situations become multiplied when his pursuers are tyros, while there is no serious danger owing to the rifles held in reserve by adjacent friends. The bear is reputed to have no chest bone; his lungs are therefore a very vulnerable point. He is also said to hug his victims to death, but such a case has never occurred to my knowledge, although it is well known that he can kill a man with one blow of his paw which is furnished with claws nearly four inches long, his chief weapons of offence. When he seizes a man, in addition to clawing him about the head and body, he uses his teeth and inflicts terrible wounds about the arms and shoulders; but the victim often recovers, as pyæmia seldom sets in, owing to the absence of the virus which usually accompanies those inflicted by a tiger or panther.

CHAPTER IV.

THE PANTHER (*Felis pardus*).

Distribution of—Varieties of—Black panther at Santawerry—Panthers at Secunderabad—Sentries and panthers—Bolting panthers with dogs—The Gun Rock—Mowl Ali—Porcupines and dogs—Spearing panthers—Dangers of—Death of Colonel Nightingale—Sitting up for panthers—Shooting pits—Kill two panthers—Am charged by one—Shoot a rogue panther—Catch cheetah cub—Tame panthers—Treachery of—Climbing capabilities of—Gāras by.

In whatever part of Southern India the sportsmen may happen to be located, he will be certain before long, to encounter this formidable animal, which is far more widely distributed than the tiger, and which adapts itself more easily to the surroundings, whether they be in the middle of agricultural districts, and devoid of any jungle or other desirable stronghold, or in remote and secluded forest tracts, far from the haunts of men.

Four varieties of this animal are found in Southern India, viz.: the panther proper, a large, active, and aggressive animal, known to the native as the bōr butcha, or taindwa; the leopard or cheetah, a smaller variety of the above; the hunting leopard, smaller still, with the head and body of a cat and the legs of a greyhound; the black panther, a beautiful variety, approaching the bōr butcha in size. The word "cheetah" is applied generally to the first three of the above animals, but it is misleading, and the above classification can leave no doubt as to the nature of the animal indicated. The hunting leopard frequents open country such as rumnahs (large meadow or pasture lands) and is a comparatively rare animal. I have occasionally seen them when stalking antelope, their natural prey, but have never fired at one, they run like lightning for 250 yards or so, no animal can touch them in speed for this distance; and they are tamed and trained to catch antelope, by the nobles of Hyderabad (Deccan), and native chieftains in other parts of India. The black panther is only to be found in hilly ground, at elevations of not less than 3000 feet. I have never shot one, although chances occasionally occurred of doing so in the hills of Southern and Western India. The first I ever saw was on the Baba Booden hills, in Mysore. We were beating for a tiger at the time, and I saw what was apparently one of the large black monkeys of the hills coming over some rocks in my front not forty yards off. As these monkeys were old acquaintances I did not examine my friend closely, and only discovered what he was, as he dashed past into a thick patch of jungle, giving me no time to fire, which I would certainly have done, even at the risk of losing the tiger, had his identity been earlier known. The panther and cheetah frequent rocky ground, cairns, heaps of boulders, and sometimes shady nullahs, in the neighbourhood of villages as a rule, where they can pick up pariah dogs, goats, different sorts of young cattle, and an occasional child. They are frequently found in such places in the open country, far from any jungle. They are very partial to pork, and porcupine flesh, and manage to catch considerable numbers of peafowl and monkeys, so their bill of fare is an extensive one. At Secunderabad, in the Deccan, they were given to plundering hen roosts, and were often shot in the act, for if their first visit was successful they were certain to return, when a charge of large shot out of a smooth bore was generally efficacious, the range being short, and the danger of bullets flying about cantonments being thus obviated. Our sentries often fired at them at night, but never with any result beyond that of scaring the intruder. On these occasions they were always described as being tigers of prodigious size and terrific aspect.

When I joined my regiment there in 1867, the place might be described as "jungly," the intrenchments had not been constructed, so there was no obstacle to prevent wild animals from wandering through the lines at night at their own sweet will.*

In those days, our senior captain was our leading regimental sportsman ; he was master of the Secunderabad hounds, and, in addition, had a private pack consisting of several courageous pariahs (curs), and some half-bred bull dogs. With these, we used to draw the caves in the isolated hills adjoining Cantonments, and frequently found and had good sport with panthers, cheetahs, and hyenas; the sportsmen being posted on "coigns of vantage" near the caves, the dogs were loosed, and very soon found out any lurking jānwar (wild beast).

It resembled ferreting rabbits on a large scale, tremendous barking and subterranean convulsions being followed by the burst of the panther, with the uninjured members of the pack in hot pursuit. Those who got the chance then loosed off their rifles, as it was invariably snap

* A large tract of scrub jungle lies five miles north of Trimulgherry, which is connected with a rocky ridge in Cantonments, by mango and toddy topes, and isolated patches of jungle; the panthers were supplied from that district.

shooting, and we seldom scored. The jãnwar would then take up a fresh position in some other cave hard by, and the process would continue—fireworks being used when the dogs failed.

The Gun Rock was a favourite draw on these occasions, it was a more or less globular hill of igneous origin — trap or basalt, about eighty feet high, over which large boulders were scattered here and there, forming caves, in fact it was the usual type of Deccan hill.

The regimental bazaar was close by, and our bungalows only a few hundred yards from its base. We often wondered that no accidents were occasioned by the projectiles discharged from its summit, and which, having missed the panthers, must have gone buzzing through our lines. It was crowned by a rock resembling a huge gun, which gave it its name. Further off, and to the north, lay Chota Mowl Ali, a larger hill of the same class, and at its base a large pile of rocks, which was also a sure find. About three miles to the east lay the town of Mowl Ali, at the foot of a similar hill, the top crowned by a temple or shrine of great sanctity, to which the devout Mahommedans of Hyderabad were in the habit of making pilgrimages. A mile beyond this was a large pile of rock, containing many " guvvies " or caves—our best draw for a panther, but occasionally tenanted by porcupines, from whose quills the dogs suffered more than from the panthers' claws. On the last occasion, four of the best dogs came to grief—one was killed on the spot, and the others had to be carried home, two afterwards succumbing to their wounds.*

* The quills had penetrated several inches, and in some cases large portions were left in the wounds.

In those days the Hyderabad State Railway had not even been commenced — the nearest station being at Sholapore, 200 miles distant, by a bad road ; nor were the cavalry and artillery barracks completed at Bolarum. An officer of the Royal Engineers, who was employed in the Public Works Department, had made arrangements for setting panther traps in the jungle-covered tracts of country ten miles north of Trimulgherry (famous as being the haunt of the terrible man-eater of Bogarum). They were strongly constructed, on the box trap principle, and baited with a kid or pariah dog. When a panther was caught, the traps were lifted on to a country cart, and brought bodily into Cantonments. On more than one occasion three panthers were thus brought in, and two at a time were by no means uncommon, as at least half a dozen traps were always kept set. The majority of animals caught were leopards—about 30 per cent. only being panthers proper—the hunting leopard was never taken in these contrivances. Word was then immediately sent round to the several regiments, stating the time and place at which the captives would be enlarged for spearing purposes.

On arrival at the meet, which was usually on the open ground north of Chota Mowl Ali — where the cavalry barracks now stand, all competitors were placed under the command of an experienced pig-sticker, whose functions were to see that nobody started until he gave the command to " Ride," by which time the panther was generally about fifty yards clear of the trap, and one hundred yards from the spears, which usually numbered a dozen.

Of course the first spear was the desideratum of all, and this was taken time after time by the sons of the

Rissaldar Major,* of the Contingent cavalry—all light weights and splendidly mounted—we heavier Europeans, on slower horses, could not touch them. Although the first spear had all the glory, those that followed had all the danger, for the panther, being as a rule only slightly wounded, crouched and sprang on every horse that approached him, generally missing the rider, but landing on the horse's hind quarters, and clawing them very severely.

Thrilling incidents were not unusual; for instance, the first time the experiment was tried of enlarging a panther, on emerging from the trap he turned round and tackled his emancipator—a soldier in my regiment—who, however, beat him off till help arrived, when he was driven off, luckily without doing any damage, and was subsequently speared. On another occasion the panther had been slightly speared, and immediately crouched ready to spring; Captain Way, of the Contingent, then rode at him, but his horse came down, shooting his rider close to the beast, which sprang forward to attack him, but was turned by Colonel Nightingale, the famous tiger shooter, who missed spearing him. I was close behind, and before Nightingale could pull round, the brute was cleverly speared by Lieutenant Warner, 4th Light Cavalry. Immediately afterwards Colonel Nightingale dropped forward in his saddle, as if shot—it was an apoplectic stroke, and the poor fellow never recovered consciousness; he was carried to the Residency, and expired in a few hours.

At another of these functions the cheetah, on being

* A native officer of field rank—a good soldier and sportsman. He had three sons in the regiment, and owned many troop horses in it.

JUST IN TIME.

enlarged, turned round and charged the wrong way into a crowd of spectators; the confusion was immense, but the brute was pluckily tackled by some terriers, and was finally speared. A few months later, an officer of the 18th Hussars was badly mauled, and these performances were stopped.* Panthers are usually shot by bolting them, as already described, with fireworks, from their strongholds in the rocks, and are often ousted in this way when beating for tigers or bears. They are fond of basking on rocks near their caves in the morning and evening sun, and may then be stalked without much difficulty. A pair of tennis shoes will be found most useful for this work; the indiarubber soles make no noise and afford good foothold on slanting rocks; the scraping of nailed boots against the stones, &c., soon alarms the jānwar. More panthers and cheetahs are, however, shot over a kill than in any other way, as they are almost certain to return about dusk if much of the animal remains uneaten; they are far more suspicious than tigers under these circumstances, and before approaching they will often lie down some distance off for several minutes, keeping a sharp look out all round; the sportsman must therefore be correspondingly cautious.

Another device is to tie up a kid near their haunts, forming an ambuscade close by; the cries of the kid are sustained by tying a string to its ear and pulling it occasionally; the panther will often charge out and spring on it immediately the coast is clear.

On killing an animal, the first thing a tiger or panther does after drinking the blood is to drag the body to some shady spot close by before devouring it, but it often

* They have since been renewed, but are often accompanied by dangerous—and even fatal—accidents.

happens that they are interrupted before they can effect this, either by the cattle herds, or by the remainder of the animals themselves if they are buffaloes, and in such cases the gāra remains in the open.

If there is no rock or tree within easy range a pit should be dug within thirty yards of the kill, on the side remote from where the jānwar is expected, a portion of the excavated soil being made into a small mound to screen the firer's head and shoulders; this mound should not exceed one foot in height—or eighteen inches at the outside—so as to resemble the excavations made by wild pigs when searching for roots—which are to be seen in most jungles—a few tufts of grass or stones being placed to make it resemble the adjoining ground if necessary, and some short but strong branches laid in position at the back of the mound capable of being moved, so as to protect the occupant in the event of the brute being wounded and making for him. These cages were much used by natives in the Kadoor district some years ago, and gave moral support, if nothing more. Ambuscades should only be resorted to when the rocks or jungles cannot be properly beaten.

An amusing incident occurred to a captain in my regiment, when quartered at Trimulgherry, whose shikari brought news of a leopard, which he stated he had seen basking that morning at the Mowl Ali rocks. About 4 p.m. he rode out, purchased a goat, and, sending his horse home, entered an ambuscade which had been made by the shikari, whom he also sent away to some distance, with orders not to return till ten o'clock, unless he heard a shot. No shot was fired, so at 10 p.m. the shikari approached, and found his sahib asleep, and the goat killed and eaten. One morning, at Bokur, our head shikari came in to report that although there had been no gāra, some panthers had been seen in a nullah about two koss (four miles) off, and that we could beat it without disturbing any of the jungles where our buffaloes were tied up for tigers; we accordingly sent for beaters, and rode out to the spot—a large and shady nullah, from which smaller ravines branched off towards the watersheds on each side. We drew lots for places as usual, and Poulton got the centre post, over the large nullah; Manley about eighty yards to his left, and I on some high ground on the right. About one hundred yards to my front a ravine ran down the slope to the big nullah, and two panthers soon emerged from it, one of which turned down the hill towards Poulton, the other coming straight towards me for a short distance, then turned down the hill also, but stopped for a moment when about eighty yards to my left-front. Seeing it was my only chance, I fired, and he rolled over quite dead, the bullet, a spherical one, passing through his heart. He was only a leopard, and it was a lucky shot, considering the size of the mark and its distance; the other one managed to sneak past Poulton without being seen, but was marked into the lower end of the nullah, so we sent the beaters round to bring it back towards us. In this beat I was posted over the nullah, and Poulton at the edge of a ravine about eighty yards to my right-front. A very large panther soon appeared above Poulton, trotting down the slope towards me; he suddenly stopped to listen to the beaters, and was polished off by him with two shots. He was a splendid specimen of the panther proper, nearly as big as a tigress, with a bull-doggy head, massive shoulders, and beautifully spotted skin. About the same time a third panther broke away far to our right, and entered a long strip of tree jungle on some rocky rising ground, half a mile off. We accordingly sent the beaters to the farther end, and took up our positions, I at the edge of a rocky ravine near the top of the ridge, Poulton and Manley farther down the slope, and below the ravine. Immediately the beat commenced there was shouting of "pedda puli" (tiger), and tremendous excitement among the beaters, and the stops along the top of the ridge cried out "he is going forward," but it turned out to be the panther we were in search of. He came lobbing along through the jungle, and stopped when abreast of me on the sky line. I fired, but the bullet struck low and too far back; he turned round and bit savagely at the wound, and then charged towards the line of beaters, growling as he ran; they were about one hundred and twenty yards off, and I shouted "take care, he is going back;" but, lead by the shikaries firing blank cartridge, they behaved splendidly, and held their ground with immense uproar. After going a short distance the brute disappeared in a patch of long grass and rocks; I then altered my position to get a better view of the ground in front, and got on the trunk of a small tree which grew close to the edge of the ravine, and bent over it; the footing was precarious, but it gave me a slightly better command of the ground—the ravine was precipitous, and at least thirty feet in depth, but if I fell it would be on the bank, and just clear of the brink.

Presently the panther again came forward at a gallop; seeing me, he altered his course and charged, growling, his tail held well aloft. I had only time to fire in his face, the recoil knocked me off the tree, and he galloped over me, merely brushing the rifle aside, which I held up to protect me. It was a clean miss, but the smoke must have blinded him, for he did not lay a claw on me, but continued his wild career, and we never saw him again. Sore in mind and body, I limped down the hill to my com-

CHARGE OF THE BOKUR PANTHER.

panions, who did not improve matters by assuring me that it was such a pretty sight to see the charge, the puff of smoke, and final collapse. About a week afterwards we were beating for a panther which had been committing depredations at a village further to the north; he was a crafty brute, and had twice evaded us by quitting the jungle before reaching the guns, and making off across the open country; but on this occasion we put more stops with rattles on the flanks, and took up a different line nearer the kill, which was one of our buffaloes, and had been intended for tigers. I was on the extreme right, at the edge of a broad stretch of open ground, and soon saw a lot of crows mobbing something out in the grassy plain, about forty yards to my right, which turned out to be our friend; the bullet broke his off fore leg, as he crawled along, close to the ground, whereupon he crouched, and began to look up into the trees for his enemy; but the left barrel caught him in the right spot at the same moment as he saw me; up went his tail in the air, a few frantic bounds towards me, and over he rolled stone-dead. He was a very old panther, with hardly a sound tooth in his head, and had been living for several years on the village products, from children down to dogs. The natives were delighted, and I told them that they might thank their crows for the result. A few days later a village shikari brought news of two cheetahs in a "guvvey" (cave) near the camp, so we sallied forth, but only to find that they were too small to shoot; we then decided to catch them alive, but this was no easy job, for they were regular little demons, and made short charges at us. Eventually we had to spear one in self-defence (although he was not much bigger than a cat), and with infinite trouble secured the other by snaring, and then, rolling him up in a cumbley (blanket), we took him to camp and put him in a rough cage, which was carried about with us from place to place, but he was too old to tame, and gradually pined away and died. A brother officer had a tame one which he had caught when very young, and which was kept chained to a box in a corner of his compound. It was very fond of being caressed, and was apparently of a gentle and amiable disposition, till one day in Burmah, an old woman who was gathering sticks came within range, when the brute sprang upon her and knocked her down, biting her badly. She was rescued by a syce, but subsequently died of her wounds and the effects of the shock. Panthers can never be trusted, they have the reputation of being more treacherous than tigers. This one, after various escapades, was brought home and presented to the Zoological Gardens, Regent's Park. All experienced sportsmen who have written about shikar, declare that the panther is a more dangerous animal than the tiger, being pluckier and more crafty, while in agility they are far superior to the striped cat. Native shikaries, too, share this belief, but on the other hand very few men escape with their lives from the clutches of a tiger, whereas it is rather exceptional to hear of a fatal accident when a panther is the aggressor—except when pyæmia ensues.

In all cultivated parts of Southern India the villagers construct mechauns—called munchals in Mysore—in the grain fields, which are platforms fixed on poles, and often more than twenty feet above the ground. From these the watchers scare away any game which may come to eat the grain at night, or, rather, they try to do so, by blowing horns, firing blank cartridge, and shouting, but in a short time the game—from elephant down to antelope—get accustomed to this reception, and decline to be ousted until stronger measures are adopted. In some districts, however, the panthers kill many of these poor people, their excellent powers of climbing enabling them to reach the platforms without difficulty.

It is strange how wild animals in a certain locality seem to adopt any bad habit started by one of their fraternity—their leader of fashion in fact—the bears for instance, in some parts of the Central Provinces, kill many natives every year, apparently because it is the fashion to do so, for they do not eat them.

Again, I remember, in the year 1870, a hilly district not far from Kurnool being so infested by man-eating tigers, that the Madras Government offered a reward of Rs.300 for every tiger that was shot there; but the jungle was very feverish and dense, as well as being difficult of access, and the tigers triumphed for many years.

INCIDENT NEAR MOWL ALI.

CHAPTER V.

THE PANTHER (*Felis pardus*).

Distinctive markings—Three cubs caught—Charge by boar—The Jamakapett panther—Munchipa—Our goats killed—Dacoits' cave—Affray with cheetah—Stirring him up—Patterson's panther—Sad accident to a beater—Panther enters my tent — Man-eating panther — The Loashera panther — The Parvutgherry panther — The Raghear panther—Panther in the Billiga Rungum Hills—Not likely to decrease in numbers — Annamullay panthers — The Bolarum bogus panther—The stalker stalked—Gāras by panther—Nocturnal depredation of—Braining panthers.

An examination of a panther skin will show that the spots—or rather rosettes—are arranged in rows corresponding to the stripes on a tiger's skin, the difference between these animals being hard to discern at distances over thirty yards—thus the large panther is often mistaken for a tiger. In the case of the leopard, his size would disclose his identity, the lines of rosettes, too, are less clearly defined, while the hide of the hunting leopard is marked with black spots alone.

Since writing the preceding chapter on the panther, I have been informed that the classification therein adopted corresponds with Jerdon's in his "Mammals of India," and with the opinions of the late Captain Forsyth, the talented author of the "Highlands of Central India."

One morning Poulton and I went out to shoot bears, and on the way to our posts a cheetah with two young ones was put up, at which he got a snap shot but missed. With much trouble we then caught the youngsters, and decided to have an extemporary beat with a few scouts and shikaries for their mother. During the beat a grand old boar was started, and came down an open slope on which I was posted. I thought he would swerve on seeing me; not a bit of it, he came at me straight as an arrow. Poulton, who was about forty yards to my left front, shouted "Fire—he's charging you." We fired simultaneously; both bullets struck him, and he rolled over dead within a few feet of me. He was a splendid old chap, with handsome tushes, and deserved a better fate. At Jamakapett we had a casual beat one day. A panther was soon turned out, at which Poulton fired several snap shots, but declared he had missed. I had great faith in his shooting, and insisted on tracking it up, soon finding slight traces of blood, till at length we arrived at the foot of an almost vertical rock twenty feet high, over which the tracks led. On seeing this we came to the conclusion that it was useless to proceed any further, as no badly wounded animal could surmount such an obstacle. However, we had just one look "for luck" round the opposite side, and discovered a cave, from which a series of sepulchral growls emanated, which increased in intensity as we advanced.

With both barrels cocked I carefully entered, and discovered that the brute was lying under a big rock within five yards. The light was good, but we could not get a glimpse of him although we pelted stones to provoke a charge. Manley then thought he would like to have a peep, and took my place. He was promptly charged, but brained the brute—a leopard—close to the muzzle of his rifle. Poulton's bullet had struck it in the belly and too far back.*

At Munchipa panthers were prowling round our camp all night and killed both our milch goats; and, as there was no news of tigers, we determined to have a beat for them. It was a terribly hot day, and, as we had been waiting for nearly two hours at our posts, we were on the point of leaving to ascertain the cause of delay, when two natives, suddenly dashing out of a large cairn of rocks in front, bolted past us as hard as they could, heading towards the jungle behind. Baliyah, at the same instant jumping on a rock, shouted in Hindustani, "Shoot the murderers," "Shoot the thieves," "Don't let them escape." The beaters also now appeared close behind Baliyah, and joined in the chorus, but of course we did not comply with their request. Baliyah now explained that the runaways were part of a band of robbers, who had been plundering and murdering travellers in that district for some weeks; that he only heard of their being in the cairn at the beginning of the beat, and decided to advance without making a noise and endeavour to catch or shoot them. We searched the cairn and collected some hundreds of rupees worth of heterogeneous property, which was placed under charge of a police peon, and a report sent to Indore of the occurrence. Next morning I sent a Hindustani letter to the tālookdar explaining the affair. This must have been forwarded to Hyderabad, as subsequently a very complimentary parchment certificate arrived from the Dewān, the late Sir Sālār Jung.

* A *post-mortem* revealed three unborn cubs, about the size of rats, which, although devoid of hair, bore the marks of all the rosettes very clearly.

One evening, on the return from an unsuccessful day's beating for a tiger, we had a short beat for a cheetah, which had been seen to enter some rocks. It was driven out towards Manley, who fired and wounded it in a leg. It then came on, rather wide to my left, at the other side of a ridge in front, which concealed it from view. The shikaries shouted "Run forward and fire." I accordingly ran up the rising ground, and on arriving at the top saw him standing under a tree close to me, and, throwing up my rifle, fired as he bounded away. He was hard hit, for he roared for quite half a minute in a thick clump of bushes close by, in which it was impossible to see him. My companions now came up, and after a short search were for going home, but we had one more look round, and soon found plenty of blood, which we followed up for some distance, and tracked him into a cave, where we could see his tail appearing from under a rock at the further end of a natural pit or arena, some ten yards square, formed by boulders which sloped steeply down. We decided to stir him up with a long pole, so sending Baliyah round for this purpose, under the protection of Manley's rifle, Poulton and I took up positions at each side of the arena. We were all suffering from the effects of the sun, which had been terribly hot all day, but the fun kept us going, for at intervals the stirring-up process provoked charges into the arena, which were always stopped by Poulton or me, by blazing into the brute's face, although, as a matter of fact, we never hit him. It was dark now, so a fire was lighted behind his stronghold, but he still held out, charging at intervals. At length I was let down into the pit by ropes, under cover of Poulton and Manley's rifles, and soon saw my friend pointing me, and brained him by the light of the fire. During a shooting trip in Western Mysore, with the late Captain Patterson, of my regiment, we were frequently disturbed at night by panthers prowling around our tents, but, owing to the dense jungle, we seldom got a chance at them in the day time, although frequently put up when driving for sambur and spotted deer. We usually went out stalking at daybreak, and Patterson one morning discovered a cheetul that had just been killed by a panther, and was still quivering. He waited some time in a tree close by, but nothing appeared, and, as it was 9 a.m. in the month of April, and the sun high and hot, he returned to camp. About 4 p.m. he was again in position, and after a short interval he saw the cheetah come down through the jungle some distance off, and commence to patrol from side to side before approaching nearer. It then laid down and watched the kill for several minutes, when, evidently being satisfied that all was well, it rose, and advancing to the dead deer, was rolled over by a bullet through the heart from Patterson's smooth bore. Shortly after this occurrence a sad accident happened in the neighbouring district. A young fellow, just out from England, and whom we had met at a sambur drive at Kulhutty, went out to shoot a panther, which had been marked into a nullah. He wounded it, and the beaters were thereupon charged by the infuriated animal, which singled out one man and chased him past the sahib.

He fired at the panther as it was in the act of springing on the unfortunate man—and shot the latter; the panther escaped.

One night in camp at Tooprany, near Hyderabad, I was awoke by a tremendous scuffling in the tent among some dogs which I had chained to my bed-cot. It sounded as if they were "woolling" some big animal within a yard of me, my bed being upset in the struggle. I jumped up and saw a shadowy form vanish in the darkness. On striking a light, two of the dogs were found to be badly mauled, one dying shortly afterwards. The miscreant was a panther, whose large pugs were visible in the sand next morning, and which had the cheek to come inside the tent for the dog, which he would certainly have carried off but for the chain. Man-eating panthers are rare, but they do exist, and are just as bad as tigers. All panthers, great and small, are, however, very much given to carrying off children. When at Chickmoogloor, in Mysore, news arrived one day that a panther had attacked and killed a native who was working on a road. His brother, only a short distance off, hearing the shrieks, ran up and killed the brute with an axe, but received such severe wounds that he too died shortly afterwards. His next of kin brought the skin to the Deputy Commissioner's office, and got the reward of fifteen rupees given by the Maharajah's government. The most exciting encounter I ever had with a panther was at Loashera, in the Neermul district, in 1871. We had been skirmishing with a bear in the fore-noon, which my friends Poulton and Manley had pursued on horseback, with intent to spear, as detailed in Chapter II., I remaining to watch a panther which had been dislodged by the bear, and was slightly wounded by a ricochet bullet in the ball of the foot. Manley having returned after the lapse of an hour, it fell to my lot to tackle the panther, which had meanwhile been spotted by the shikaries crouching under a rock in an adjacent cave. On entering it, there was the panther sure enough, with great luminous eyes, crouching within a few feet, and apparently ready to spring. The entrance was very narrow and cramped, a projecting rock preventing the rifle from being brought to the right shoulder; indeed, it was necessary to crane round the edge of this, in order to see the brute. I could not shoot from the left shoulder with any certainty, nor were the circumstances favourable for experiments, so I determined to attack from another point. Going round to the back of the cairn, I entered a branch of the cave on my hands and knees, and, creeping forward, came upon him from the rear. The light was very bad, but he was within a yard of me, so, placing the muzzle of the rifle within a few inches of the root of his tail, I fired with the intention of raking him from end to end.

He roared and rushed out of the cave, and I retreated backwards on all fours nearly stifled with smoke and filth, the cave being evidently a favourite retreat of all kinds of jānwars. Emerging from the cave, I reloaded, and climbed up a rock near its mouth, whence I saw the brute crouching under a bush about fifteen yards off. I fired and he came at me like a flash of lightning. He was almost touching the muzzle when the left barrel was loosed; his impetus carried him on, and striking the muzzle he sent me flying head over heels into a seega kye (wait-a-bit thorn) bush.* The natives preferring to witness the scene from a distance, it gave me much trouble to get out of this unassisted; but the hook-shaped thorns were at length negotiated, and I emerged like a hedgehog covered with spines. The panther had been marked into an adjacent fissure, and out he came at me again as fresh as paint, but this time a shot between the eyes rolled him over. Up he got again and struggled towards me, but I now tackled him with a hog spear and polished him off. The ricochet shot had only inflicted a flesh wound in the foot. The "raking" shot—a hollow pointed bullet propelled by

* Acacia or mimosa.

DEATH OF THE LOASHERA PANTHER.

$2\frac{1}{2}$ drachms of powder (an absurd charge)—had only penetrated a few inches and mushroomed against the thigh bone; the third shot struck just behind the heart, the fourth made a huge but shallow wound in the throat, the fifth between the eyes carried away the lower part of the brain pan, and would ultimately have killed him, but the spear was quite necessary. The natives were in great delight, as the beast was supposed to have killed and eaten a boy, who was herding goats within fifty yards of the spot two days previously.

In the hot weather of 1881 my colonel and I were returning to Secunderabad from a shooting trip, with a view to finishing our leave at Ootacamund on the Neilgherry Hills, and were anxiously looking forward to the cool breezes of the blue mountains. We were encamped at Parvutgherry, at one time a very favourite spot for tigers, and were on the point of starting one morning for Raepurty, when news arrived of a gāra, so we sent on our tents and baggage, retaining our horses and a pad elephant.

Beaters were obtained with some difficulty, as two men had been killed there by a wounded tiger some years before when a sahib had been shooting, and the fact was still fresh in the minds of the villagers. However, we collected about thirty, and started on our horses for the scene of the kill, which was about two miles off. On the way we met Kistiah, the head shikari, who reported that the gāra was the work of a bōr butcha, and that while examining it, the brute had appeared in an evidently aggressive humour; whereupon he had fired at and wounded it, and it had then disappeared into the jungle. We got our rifles and approached the kill, but the panther was nowhere to be seen, so, deciding to continue our researches on the pad elephant, it was brought up and we mounted, having settled that the Colonel was to be responsible for anything that appeared on the port side, while I looked after the starboard. We had not gone forty yards when I saw something white move under a tree close to me; it was the panther's belly, and I immediately fired; he rolled over growling and biting the ground, and expired in a few seconds. The Express bullet made a wound as large as the palm of my hand; it looked as though a shell had burst on the skin, the reason being that the brute was end on when I fired. We waited a short time before approaching the body, and I pointed out the wound to my chief, who declared he thought it was a flower which had dropped from an overhanging kino tree! It turned out to be a leopard, and we were surprised that so small an animal should attack and kill a full grown buffalo. We then returned to camp, represented by a shady peepul tree, had a scratch breakfast, followed by an awful ride in the hot sun to Raepurty, where we arrived about 5 p.m. A few nights after, at Ragheer, a panther patrolled round the camp for several hours, making night hideous with a noise resembling a cross-cut saw drawn through a plank of wood. We had given directions to be called at four o'clock to go out to shoot bears; but Kistiah, who judged his time by the stars, awoke us at 1 a.m. This disconcerted us a good deal, and, being unable to sleep, owing to the panthers' lullaby, we started about three o'clock and reached the caves before daylight, but the bears had returned before our arrival, as we discovered by their tracks. On returning to camp I saw the panther basking on a rock in the morning sun, and, sending one of the elephants which had come to meet us, to distract its attention, stalked to within ninety yards, fired, and missed him clean. I found the mark of the bullet on a rock behind where the panther had been reclining, just a few inches too high.

My next adventure with a basking panther was a few months later on the Billiga Rungum Hills in Mysore; but on that occasion I got within thirty yards of him after an easy stalk. Whatever may happen to the tiger, in view of the increasing use of firearms by natives, and the greater facilities of transport by railways, which have brought hitherto secluded jungles to within a few hours of many stations, no fears need be entertained that the panther will be exterminated; they are crafty, and too well able to take care of themselves, difficult to force from their fastnesses, which abound all over the country; and their depredations, being generally confined to goats, dogs, and such small deer, do not bring them so much before the eye of the public. Their favourite haunts in the Annamullays were in the vicinity of the Ibex hills, but they, as well as tigers, very soon found out the dead bodies of any bison that might have been shot in the lower part of the forest, and, by stalking up to these, a shot was not unfrequently obtained, as they generally lay up close by, and when started, would bound away for thirty or forty yards, and stop to have a look at the intruder, thus giving a fair opportunity for a successful shot. In bygone years at Secunderabad, one day during a big luncheon at our mess, news was brought by an orderly of the Contingent, that a panther in the Bolarum Cantonments had killed and eaten a cow, and had afterwards been marked down in some adjacent rocks. All the leading sportsmen of the station happened to be present, Colonel Nightingale of the Contingent, and Captain Hazelrigg of my regiment being regarded as representatives of the Indian and British armies respectively. It was agreed that two shikar elephants should be sent for, and that the panther should be tackled after the tiffin, by our respective doughty champions, the remainder of the party being spectators, to learn how to do the thing properly. Accordingly we all rode out to the trysting-place near Bolarum, where the two elephants were in readiness. Just as we arrived, a sowar* came galloping up to report that, not only had he seen the panther in the rocks, but that it had chased him across the plain, and it was only his horse's fleetness that saved his life. He added, that, on being foiled, the brute, had returned to his lair in the rocks. On hearing this, the rival competitors, thirsting for the fray, pushed their elephants forward, and a race ensued. The colonel's elephant was the slower, and his unfortunate mahout had a bad time from the stock of his rifle, as Hazelrigg gradually surged ahead. Arriving within fifty yards of the rocks, the panther was soon descried on a ledge at the foot of a boulder, crouching, and ready to spring. Hazelrigg being first up, fired at the brute, but evidently missed, for it did not move. At this moment Nightingale arrived and delivered his fire with like result. More shots were fired by both, but the panther took no notice and still remained crouching, till at length a shot from Hazelrigg rolled it off the ledge. With a loud shout of triumph, and amid tremendous applause from the "gallery," he pushed his elephant up to the lifeless body, but only to find that it was a skin stuffed with straw. The spectators were at first perplexed, and finally convulsed with laughter; not so the principals, who swore that they would have the originator "out" and shoot him! But they never discovered his identity—he was a gallant officer of a corps not much given to practical joking, viz., the Royal

* Native trooper.

Engineers. The most amusing part of the story is the sowar's report of his escape, it is so like what a native would state under the circumstances.

One morning I was out stalking spotted deer in a bamboo jungle near Atticulpoora, in Southern Mysore, when, on rounding a clump of canes, we saw a rival sportsman in the form of a panther, who was evidently bent on the same game, about seventy yards distant, on a large rock, and scanning the jungle all around. My face and body were shaded by a branch, through which I was peeping, but, on stepping back to hold a council of war, he must have seen my legs move, and have mistaken them for a deer, for down he dropped stealthily to the ground, and began to stalk me, creeping quickly along for about ten yards at a time towards me, and then crouching behind any available covert; in this way he reached a large bamboo, about forty yards distant. After anxiously awaiting his reappearance for some minutes, I decided to return the compliment by stalking him, but it was in vain; he must have discovered his mistake, and retired unobserved, for the spot was vacated when examined by me. The panther commences to eat the flank of any animal he may have killed, thence extending his operations to the stomach and entrails. He is a much bolder animal than the tiger when in search of prey, being more accustomed to the presence of man from his habit of infesting village outskirts. He frequently enters them at night to look for dogs or other domestic animals, and will then even scratch through the roof of a hut to get at his victims.

A good opportunity for a braining shot is more often offered by a panther or leopard than by other animals coming under the heading of big game, the nature of the sport being conducive to close quarters, among heaps of boulders or large rocks, under which he is much given to squatting, and where he may be approached to within a few yards, care being taken to be out of reach of the final spring, which usually follows the shot. The line of his body will indicate the direction of this, and with a shell or an express bullet, the aim need not necessarily be very true, owing to the great expansion of the projectile after impact or explosion. A side shot is the best position, as the brain offers a larger surface; if it is missed the shot may smash the spine, and the final spring will be clear of the sportsman. Nearly half my panthers and leopards were obtained thus. The panther proper must, however, be recognised on such occasions as the dangerous brute that he really is, and his attack must be as carefully conducted as if he were a tiger.

CHARGE OF THE LOASHERA PANTHER.

CHAPTER VI.

THE TIGER (*Felis tigris*).

Classification of—Taming cubs—Rāni—Becomes dangerous—Tiger at Poppinapett—Gāra at Nowsanpully—Sit up all night—A ghastly vigil—How the tiger feeds—Man-eaters different—Tigers in Annamullay—Scarcity of man-eaters—Cause of—The Poppinapett tigress—Destruction of human life by—Unsuccessful beats—Pochapooram—Eluded by man-eater—Her end—Preliminaries of shooting trip—Shamantapoor—Tying-up baits—The soup-plate wallah—Poulton's adventure—Servant bitten by snake—Close shave with cobra—Shoot bears—Kowlass—Rajah's visit—Sambur—Bear's meat—Lingumpulli man-eater—Tigress and cubs—Man-eater kills buffalo—Kola Baloo—Close quarters with man-eater—Beernecks—Tiger's fat—Posting of guns—Firing during beat.

MAN-EATERS being merely ordinary tigers that from force of circumstances, or inclination, have developed a taste for human flesh, should not be regarded as distinct from the rest of their species. Adopting, therefore, the usual classification, tigers may be divided into game-killers and cattle-lifters—the former are light active brutes, in good condition, and as hard as nails, and are usually to be found in wooded country, where game is plentiful on which they subsist; the latter is of a heavier type in every way, frequenting more thickly inhabited districts, where he levies toll on the villagers' flocks and herds—and when these are driven away to fresh pastures, he accompanies them on their travels, keeping touch of them the whole year round. If pigs or deer come in his way, he will vary his beef diet with pork or venison, but he is a comparatively clumsy beast, and the exertion of hunting these wild animals neither suits his physique nor his inclination.

A good sized cattle-lifter will measure from nine to nine and a half feet, from nose to tip of tail, and weigh over thirty stone. Measurements should be made between uprights, the contours of the body should not be followed, but they (measurements) are bad criterions of size, for many tigers of the cattle-lifter type have absurdly short tails, and a small game-killer of a little over twenty stone in weight, the possessor of a well-developed tail, may equal in length a lusty cattle-lifter of over thirty stone, that could kill and eat him. Tigresses are considerably less in both weight and length, and I have on several occasions won bets by backing seven feet nine inches against the latter.

A tigress generally has but two cubs, occasionally three. If caught when very young they can be trusted as pets up to two years old, after that they cannot be relied on, although not nearly so treacherous as panthers. The great difficulty in rearing them is the liability of milk—whether of cows or goats—to curdle after they have swallowed it—which almost invariably kills them; it ought to be diluted with half its bulk of water, but even then there is some risk. I was once staying with a friend whose menagerie consisted of a nearly full-grown tigress named Rāni, a hunting leopard, and a bear, of which the leopard was the least sociable, and the bear the most so, in fact she was a regular nuisance, her attentions were so marked and unremitting. She would not remain quiet for five minutes, being always solicitous for caresses. She had been very badly brought up, having been for more than a year chained to a tamarind tree, and regularly baited by all the curs in the neighbourhood, but this rough treatment did not seem to have any lasting effect on her temper for she subsequently became too affectionate. The tigress occasionally broke her chain and would then always make for the bungalow, emitting a rough kind of purring noise, and intensely pleased. The first time she visited me in this way, her approach was heralded by the noise of the broken chain and the loud purring. I was writing a letter when she entered the room, and began to push herself against my chair in the way a cat does when pleased, nearly sending me flying on to the floor; but a few rough words caused her to cease, and she lay quietly down by my side. All the natives had bolted on the first alarm except the syce's wife, a very plucky woman, who followed the tigress, and, on my calling, entered the room, caught the end of the chain, and walked off followed by Rāni, exactly as if she was a big cat; she was then secured without further trouble.

Rāni never showed bad temper except when feeding, when nobody dare approach her; on these occasions she would lie in a corner watching the food, which was generally cooked goat's flesh, and if anybody came near she would spring forward, growling savagely, to the full extent of the chain, which luckily never gave way in these rather critical circumstances. One day, wrapping myself in a tiger skin, I went to see her; much to my surprise, instead of being delighted she became perfectly paralysed with fear, and rushed into a corner, trembling all over. Soon after this she again broke her chain, and, seeing a cow belonging to a bheestie (water-carrier) in the compound, stalked and killed it, being recaptured and chained with difficulty. Her disposition completely changed shortly afterwards, and it became evident she could no longer be trusted, so her ultimate destination was the Dewan's zoological gardens at Hyderabad, to which place also the bear was consigned. The first tiger I ever saw in the jungle, was at Nowsanpully in June, 1868, where a brother officer and I were encamped for several days, having tied up young buffaloes at all the likely places between that village and Poppinapett, a few miles distant. This district was the favourite resort of a tigress, which was far too cunning to kill our ties, although she was in the habit of inspecting them, as was proved by her tracks. After waiting in vain for several days for a gāra (kill) we decided to have a chance beat, as our patience was exhausted. Although she eventually became a notorious man-eater, her victims up to that time had only amounted to two cattle herds, one of whom had ventured to peep into a cave where she was unfortunately at home, whereupon she sprang out and killed him; the other man was walking through the jungle, when the brute appeared and killed him without any provocation, but in neither case did she eat the bodies.

I well remember being posted on the ground in front of the above mentioned cave that day, and making schemes for my defence in case the enemy appeared. A small bush screened me in front; there were two avenues of approach from the jungle, one on each side, and an open space, about twenty yards broad, between the bush and the edge of the jungle. I decided to fire at the head directly it appeared (which it luckily did not)—there was no other alternative.

Our camp at Nowsanpully lay close to a range of rocky hills interspersed with scrub jungle, about two miles long and one broad, a very tigerish-looking spot, and connected with some similar ground a koss (two miles) distant, by straggling patches of scrub jungle and rocks at intervals.

We used to go out in the mornings after bears, and fish during the day in a deep bowrie (well) close to our tents, which were pitched under some mango trees. The haylas (young buffaloes) were tied up some distance off, so there was nothing to prevent our shooting small game near camp. On the morning of the 4th June I had shot a bear, and had also made an unsuccessful rush to intercept a tiger (as already described under the heading of "bears"), and the following day went out to look for some partridges for the pot. About 11 a.m., on my way back to camp, the shikari came running up to report that the tiger had killed a bāil (ox), and was eating it within a short distance of the village. My friend and I were soon on the spot, and found that, in the interim, the tiger had dragged the gāra under a big rock, towards which we advanced, on the look out for squalls. We had just sighted the head of the bāil when we were suddenly stopped by two deep growls, and the tiger moved slowly away, as could be seen by the bushes and grass shaking, as she brushed through them; we jumped up on the adjacent rocks, but could not get a glimpse of the brute. After inspecting the gāra, which bore the marks of teeth and claws in the neck near the shoulder, and of which part of the buttocks had been eaten, we decided to sit up over the kill that night. It was bright moonlight, and we watched in vain till about 1 o'clock a.m., when the moon became obscured by clouds, and the tiger returned and had a hearty meal within ten yards of the rock on which we were seated. We could hear the crunching of the bones, but never a sight of her did we get; if we had done so, it might have been the means of saving the lives of more than one hundred natives which were subsequently killed and eaten by her. During the tiger's repast a heavy shower of rain came on, but when the moon reappeared she was gone, and, although we sat there till 9 a.m. it was in vain. This experience of sitting up over a kill, was only once repeated by me, over the remains of a woman which had been killed by the same tiger near Sunkerrumpett, three years after the above occurrence, but it was a ghastly vigil, and, getting sick of the business after a couple of hours' watch, I returned to camp, keeping an uncommonly sharp look-out over my shoulder; the moon was shining brightly, but it was an uncomfortable experience in every sense of the word. The tiger almost always commences its meal at the lower part of its victim's thigh, whether animal or human being, but in the latter case it sometimes begins at the feet, and devours the legs as far as the knees. A man-eater seldom returns to its kill; they are much too cunning to do so; moreover, in the case of a human being, there is little or nothing left for a second visit.

They are furnished indifferently from both types of tiger, and are as a rule tigresses, which probably contract the habit when hampered by their cubs, and obliged to kill something for them. In the Annamullays, tiger tracks were visible in many places, but the animals themselves were seldom seem. The Carders predicted that the carcases of the bison I had shot, would soon attract them to Perrincudavoo, where I was encamped at one time; and at four o'clock next morning their prophecy was fulfilled by a tiger patrolling round the camp, and roaring at intervals, but it was too dark to see him in the dense shadows of the forest trees. The only recorded case of a man-eater in those hills was at this spot, where some years previous a tiger had carried off several Carders, but it was eventually shot by Vyapoori Moopen,* after killing a pony and gorg-

* Chief of the tribe.

ing itself with flesh to such an extent, that it lay up in the jungle close to the village. These tigers had plenty of game to subsist on, and there was no excuse for their becoming man-eaters, nor were the natives in any fear of them. In March, 1871, having joined my friends Manley and Poulton at Secunderabad, we marched northward for Kowlass, and on arrival at Sunkerrumpett, determined to devote some days to the pursuit of the Poppinapett tigress, which had, as already stated, developed into an accomplished and sanguinary man-eater. Her iniquities had roused the whole district, it being reported that she had killed and eaten over one hundred human beings. But, this being the ordinary reputation of every man-eater in those parts, it cannot be implicitly relied on. Its hunting grounds stretched over a large tract of country, from a few miles south of Sunkerrumpett, to Nowsanpully (nearly twelve miles to the east as the crow flies), and extending northwards, some twenty-five miles along the Kowlass-Sunkerrumpett road. On the 3rd March it had killed a woman, towards Jogiepett—to the south of Sunkerrumpett—its previous victim near the same place being a man who had been killed a week before. Like all man-eaters it had left that district after killing, and had, in the interim favoured Nagadurra, a village seventeen miles off, with a visit. The country near Jogiepett was covered with cholum (millet) fields, but having reconnoitred it, we came to the conclusion that it would be useless and impossible to arrange a beat there. Two days after this she killed a man and a woman near Sunkerrumpett, in the direction of Nagadurra. She was accompanied by two cubs, which were receiving a nice lesson from their mother. Our haylas (young buffaloes), to the number of twenty-three, were tied up at all the likely places near water, within a radius of six miles, but as she would not touch any of them, we beat all her favourite haunts for two consecutive days on the chance of finding her, as we reasoned that the presence of her cubs would impede her, and induce her to lie up in such places. All this being in vain, we marched to Nagadurra, and as no gāras were reported, had two days' casual beating there, but no tiger appeared, although this was one of her usual halting places on the way from Sunkerrumpett; when she temporarily left that area, for fresh scenes of blood in the northern parts of her domain. On the afternoon of the second day we found three bears in a pile of rocks, and had a merry hour baiting them with fireworks, but could only get one to bolt, which came out within a yard of me, and was promptly shot by Manley. Next day, at Pochapooram, we beat a long stretch of scrub jungle and rocks, the reputed resort of the man-eater, only turning out some bears and pigs, but on the return journey to camp we were requested by the inhabitants of a village to beat an adjacent patch of rocky ground, where they stated the tigress had killed a woman not half an hour before we arrived. It was an isolated patch of scrub jungle and rocks, about two acres in extent, situated in open ground within three hundred yards of the village, and fully six hundred yards from the jungle we had been beating, which was the nearest covert. Placing stops, whose guns were loaded with blank cartridge, out in the open ground in this direction, to head the tiger back if it attempted to break there, we took up posts on suitable rocks, having directed the beaters to advance from the village end of the patch very slowly towards us, and to use plenty of rockets to clear the way. These orders were carried out to the letter, but the beat was a blank one; they were then ordered to beat it over again, but with like result, finally we (the guns) searched every foot of it with the shikaries, but no traces of the brute could be found, she must have sneaked away on our approach, but how she could have done this without being seen, was a problem we were unable to solve. The natives explained that the tigress had been seen to strike the woman down, and that about twenty of them had proceeded together to the spot, beating tom-toms (which we had heard), whereupon, having drank the blood, the brute moved into the rocky patch, not having had time to eat the body, which was then carried to the village. This was our last day in pursuit of this scourge, as our time was limited, and we had much ground before us. I never heard more about her until nine years afterwards, at Secunderabad, when inquiries resulted in news that she had been shot by a Pathan from Hyderabad, but I could not ascertain the details. At the commencement of the hot weather about the middle of March, one or more shooting parties annually left Secunderabad for the jungle lying northwards towards the River Godavery. There was room for the operation of three parties in that zone of country, without interfering with each other's sport. The mode of procedure was as follows: About Christmas time the representatives of each party having met and agreed upon their respective theatres of sport, their shikaries were despatched to the different villages to obtain news of the big game in the vicinity; they returned before the end of February bringing certificates from the head men of the various villages, stating the numbers of tigers, bears, and panthers supposed to exist in the neighbouring jungles.

The chief of each party then called its members together, and the plan of campaign was duly arranged.

Pack bullocks having been engaged—or bullock carts if the country was easy, and well provided with roads—and supplies packed, the convoy was started off under charge of a dependable man, with orders to be at a certain village, generally about fifty miles out, on the day the sahibs leave commenced. We usually had horses posted and covered this distance at one stretch.

A "tākeed" or "purwāna"* was always furnished on application to the Dewan at Hyderabad; it was merely an injunction signed by his order, to the effect that the head men of villages and other officials were held responsible, that supplies of all kinds, coolies, &c., which might be required by the sahibs were supplied to them. Without this, nothing could be obtained, and even with it we had occasional difficulty with some of the local grandees, who did not wish to admit any authority superior to their own. We were also furnished with two elephants whenever the Mahommedan feast of the Muharram had been celebrated at Hyderabad. These animals were most useful for transport purposes, and added to the prestige of the party, but with few exceptions were not staunch enough for shikār purposes.

After all the kindness evinced by His Highness the Nizam, it used to go against the grain to claim the State rewards for the tigers, panthers, bears, and hyænas, that were shot during these trips; but, as all this prize money went to the shikaries, in addition to their ordinary wages, we hardened our hearts and did violence to our feelings by signing the claims, which were invariably paid without

* We were informed that a separate tākeed would be necessary to enter the territory of Vikar-ool-Oomrah — a tributary chief, who resided at Hyderabad, and owned many tālūqs (parishes) in that state.

comment. The rewards were as follows :—Tigers, twenty Halli Sicca rupees (Hyderabad currency) ; bears, hyænas, and wolves, five each ; and panthers, ten. A few days later we arrived at Shamantapoor and pitched our camp close to a large wooded nullah where our buffaloes were tied up. The head shikari requested that one of us should accompany him when he visited these in the mornings and evenings, stating that a "very depraved" tiger was in this jungle, almost as bad as the Poppinapett fiend.

Accordingly I went out with him that afternoon, and had not gone 300 yards before we encountered two bears in the aforesaid nullah, which were allowed to go unmolested, lest the shots should scare away the tiger whose pugs were in every sandy nullah—huge ones they were too ; in fact, so large that we nicknamed him the "soup plate wallah," as they were supposed to be equal to that utensil in size. The haylas were usually tied near water, in places where it was expected the tiger would come to drink, and as he generally walks along roads or tracks in the night, the meeting of several of these was always a favourite spot for a tie. When visited, they were always foddered and watered. To secure the animal the foot was firmly tied to a stake driven into the ground, or to a bush. If tied by the head, the poor beast was liable to be strangled in its efforts to escape if the tiger approached it, which he often did without any intention of killing, and on several occasions he had evidently been playing with them, as was plainly visible by the tracks. The feelings of the unlucky hayla under these circumstances can be more easily imagined than described.

The next day Poulton visited the buffaloes accompanied by the shikari and bāil coolies carrying fodder. There was no kill, but during his afternoon round, the tiger walked past within twenty yards of him in a shady part of the nullah. He was armed with a light sporting Snider rifle, loaded with very sensitive shells, which not unfrequently burst on the skin on impact, and he therefore did not fire. We visited the spot, which gave no advantage of height or cover to the firer, and unanimously decided that he had acted wisely; with a more dependable rifle, however, the case would have been entirely different. It was marvellous how he had escaped being seen by the brute, for the tree he was standing by was not more than six inches in diameter, and there was no intervening long grass or other covert to screen him. While here, one of the servants was badly bitten by a krait—a very poisonous snake—as he was lifting a gun-case in the tent. In order to protect the leather from white ants, this had been placed on four stones, in the customary way, and the reptile had taken refuge underneath, remaining there until I killed it with a stick—it was not much over one foot in length. The wound was cauterised, and ammonia administered internally and externally; we then took the man outside and kept him running between two horsekeepers at intervals of a few minutes for over an hour, giving him nips of brandy now and then. He had got over the drowsy state by the end of that time. Half an hour afterwards we went to see how he was getting on, and found the servants had procured a native, who had the reputation of being able to charm away the effects of snake-bite. This man was hard at work waving a branch of neem tree (something like our ash) and muttering incantations. He recovered completely in the course of six hours, and no doubt the charmer got the credit of the cure.

Next morning we marched four miles to Kowlass, and had just pitched our camp on a slope near the old fort, when a coolie brought news of a gāra near Shamantapoor. After breakfast we started back, and beat unsuccessfully all day. I stepped over a cobra without seeing it, which immediately rose and struck at my gun bearer, luckily missing him, as he saw it just in time, and sprang into the air. It had been lying in some short grass at the edge of a dried up tank, and I was quite unconscious of what had occurred, until the natives shouted "Sāmp" (snake), "Khabardār, sahib" (take care, sir), when turning round I saw the gunbearer in mid-air. Only two days previously I had remarked to my shikari on passing this spot "All the snakes for a mile round have probably collected here," to which he replied "Bē shak," *i.e.*, "undoubtedly." Bears having been reported to exist in the ruins of the old fort close to camp, we went out early next morning, and had hardly been posted, when two came in straight towards Manley, who made a very pretty shot at the leader, killing him stone dead; the other broke through our line, receiving leaden contributions from each rifle, but made good his escape into the fort. After breakfast news came of another kill at Shamantapoor, but the delinquent turned out to be a panther. The town of Kowlass was situated on some rising ground, about half a mile from the glacis of the fort on which we were encamped, the intervening valley affording us our water supply. In the evening the Rajah with his retinue came to pay us a visit, bringing the customary presents of limes and sweetmeats. We were quite ashamed of our jungle get-up and disreputable appearance, when contrasted with his white linen, silken garments, and neat attire; but he was a nice gentlemanly fellow, like most of his creed, and said, in reply to our apologies, that he would have been surprised to see us in any other garments when on a jungle expedition.

Poulton shot a fine sambur next morning, the venison being very like beef in flavour and appearance, which was a welcome change from the everlasting goat's flesh and murghi (fowl). We had lately attempted to vary this with some bear's meat, but the result was disastrous and unexpected; generally speaking it is wholesome food, but on this occasion it proved quite the reverse. We missed vegetables more than anything else—one always has a great longing for them, which is seldom gratified in the jungle—exposure to the sun seeming to cause distaste for meat diet; we had, however, plenty of potatoes and pickled onions, and mainly from these, concocted an excellent salad every night for dinner. The shikaries brought in news after breakfast of a kill near Lingumpulli, a small village of some half a dozen houses, about two koss off (four miles). On arrival there we found but four beaters available, only one house being inhabited by a decrepit old man and his sons, who stated they were the sole occupants of the village, all the others having run away or been killed by the big tiger (soup-plate wallah). They declared that the tigress did no harm, but that the "burra bāgh" was a "shaitān,"* and that if their old father could have been moved from his hut they would have migrated elsewhere with their friends. The shikaries, who had been scouring the country for beaters directly they had heard of the gāra, soon arrived with about one hundred men. The scene of operations was a thickly-wooded triangular valley of about five acres in extent. From one corner a broad nullah—now dry—ran towards Kowlass; it was full of islands covered with Indian beech, caroonda bushes, palas kino trees, and long grass, and we were posted near its exit from the valley. The hills, devoid of any covert but some straggling

* The big tiger was a devil.

bushes, rose abruptly all round, and the nullah appeared to be the only spot a tiger would be likely to break from. It was a very tigerish-looking spot; many of the soft-barked trees were scored to a height of seven or eight feet, by their habit of springing up and drawing their claws through the bark to sharpen or clean them, and we found that the cubs had been at the same game too; the marks were quite fresh, so we attributed the gāra to the tigress. Immediately the beat commenced, the tigress and cubs were started, and broke away over a steep and bare hill three hundred yards to our right, passing between the stops, who were too far apart to head them, and whose rattles, though vigorously used, were of no effect.

Our syces had been left with the horses some distance off in rear, and at the end of the beat came running up to say they had just seen the big tiger killing one of our buffaloes, not a quarter of a mile off, on the bank of the large nullah we were then posted on, and that not a minute had elapsed since they saw it drinking the blood of its victim. We forthwith advanced shoulder to shoulder to the gāra, which was still quivering when we arrived. It was too late in the day to arrange a beat, so, hastily deciding to sit up close by, as the tiger was evidently within a few yards of us in the nullah, we mounted some of the adjacent trees, forming a semi-circle round the kill, the base of which was the nullah. Presently an old bear came slowly along, sniffing about the roots of the trees within twenty yards, but of course was not fired at. A "Kola baloo" * then crept out of the nullah in a cautious and scared way; looking suspiciously all round. He approached the carcase, and, after smelling it, rushed

* "Tiger's provider," a jackal that attaches himself to a tiger, and acts as scout for him.

quickly back into the nullah ; this performance was repeated several times, and no doubt he was the tiger's companion, and told him that things were not quite right; at all events, after waiting until it was too dark to see the buffalo's carcase, I whistled to my companions, this being the signal to descend. They were within forty and sixty yards respectively of my post, and, of course, in separate trees. Giving my rifle to Baliyah, I slid down the stem to the ground, and there, within five yards, was the tiger on the edge of the nullah, looking gigantic in the gloom! I kept my eyes on him, not daring to move, and said in a firm voice to Baliyah, "Bandook jaldi do" (Give the gun quickly), but he could not reach my hand with the butt. I then said, "Pukāro" (shout); he guessed what was the matter, and together we yelled in such a fashion that the brute, being scandalised, retired into the nullah. The tiger kept sniffing me at first, being, probably, equally surprised at my sudden appearance; and quite twenty seconds must have elapsed from the time of my descent until he retired. It is well on such occasions to let tigers know that there are other men about, and that they have not a solitary individual to tackle; even a man-eater recoils from attacking several men in a group; but, if hungry, it will often carry off the last man of the batch as they hurry along the haunted road.

Two small isolated bones are found in the shoulders of a tiger, named beernecks, which are greatly valued by the natives as charms, and which—as well as the whiskers—will assuredly be stolen, unless the sahib looks after them himself. They are unconnected with any other bone, being embedded in a mass of muscle, to which they probably act as supports or fulcra. The fat, too, is another product of the tiger, to which great value is attached, it

A TWILIGHT ADVENTURE.

being an excellent cure for rheumatism, to which I can personally testify. It should be melted in a saucepan and poured into bottles, which must be well corked and sealed. This will assuredly disappear even more rapidly than the whiskers and beernecks if not watched; indeed, I have never been able to secure more than ten soda-water bottles full from the fattest tiger, *i.e.*, not half the crop which ought to have been yielded by him.

The tiger being gifted with a far keener nose than he usually gets credit for, the guns should be posted to leeward whenever possible, the beaters commencing up-wind, this course being subject to local, and perhaps more important, considerations, which alone can be determined on the spot.

During the burning days, when this sport is best followed, there is often but little, if any, breeze, and, in any case, the height at which the guns are usually posted above the ground diminishes the chance of the tiger getting their wind, always provided that there is no rising ground in front and within range, in passing over which he might be on the same level as the sportsmen.

It is not customary to fire at other animals that may appear when beating for a tiger, but all the same it is frequently done without detriment to the sport, and at the worst would probably only turn him to another gun. When he is marked into a restricted area, such as a small nullah or patch of jungle, where seeing him is a certainty, it is always understood by the sportsmen that their fire is to be reserved for his exclusive benefit.

CHAPTER VII.

THE TIGER (*Felis tigris*).

Kills followed by blank beats—Reason for this—Smoothing tracks—The Poopul nullah day—Poulton's bear—Shimoga—Kills, but no tiger—Tigers in a temple—Brinjarries—Pig sticking—Bokur—Soamtanah—Scientific beat—Tiger shot—Absurd stampede—Shikari killed by tiger—Golamorra—Gāra—All miss tiger—Unpleasant predicament—Heights jumped by tiger—Death of an officer and his shikari—The tiger killed—Panthers good climbers—Aiming from trees—Major Fergusson's tiger—Apparowpett—Red ants—Fire at tiger—Yellow bees—Fire at bogus tiger—Tiger found dead—Captain Preston's accident — Makmudpully — Manley's adventure — Tigress shot — Serenade by her admirers — Tigers fond of putrid meat—A lawyer's shooting party.

One of the peculiarities of big game shooting is the fact, that although the particular jungle in which you are located may be full of the tracks of tigers, and of other kinds of big game, days of arduous work in the sun may elapse, without a shot being obtained by any of the party. Sometimes this is due to want of co-operation with the local shikaries, or of jealousy on the part of your own shikari, who may ignore the suggestions of the village men, whom he regards as clowns. Even in jungles where tigers are killing the tied-up animals almost nightly, it not unfrequently happens that the sportsmen are unable to find them, although they may beat day after day over the kills, and in the most likely places in the neighbourhood. In such cases the tiger either travels to some distant retreat, perhaps several miles off, or lies up in some secluded spot near at hand, which he has discovered by experience is secure from molestation—such as an isolated rock, clump of bushes, or patch of long grass, which has escaped the hunter's eye. When visiting the tied-up animals the shikaries always trail leafy branches along the sandy tracks in the jungle, as they walk through it; this obliterates any stale footmarks, and, if a kill occurs, often shows the course taken by the tiger after his meal, by which means he may be "ringed," or marked into a certain limited space, such as a nullah, isolated hill, or other restricted area of jungle. There are many tracts of country, however, where the ground is too hard and rocky to afford the shikaries any help in this way, and all that can then be done, is to beat the most likely places on chance. This was the case at Kowlass; we had two kills for two days in succession, after my evening *rencontre* as related in the last chapter, followed by many unsuccessful beats, and the shikaries declared it would be useless to waste more time there, as the tigers were "chōrs" (rogues). We accordingly decided to wait one day longer, and to commence by having a turn at bears in the early morning, at a place remote from our ties, named the Poopul nullah, which was five miles distant from camp.

Being without watches, we relied on the stars, and got up about 1 a.m., imagining it to be four o'clock. On arrival at our ground it was still quite dark, so we all lay down to sleep, pretty close together, as the man-eater was in the vicinity. After dozing for about two hours I arose, and caught Poulton by the foot, to awaken him, whereupon he started up, clutching his rifle, exclaiming "Oh! my God, has it come to this." He had been dreaming of the tiger, and imagined he was in his clutches!

He shot a fine male bear soon afterwards, which shammed death, and very nearly scragged him. There were no kills reported that morning, and next day we marched northwards. It is most disappointing having to leave a place where tigers are killing regularly, on account of being unable to find them. During the preceding hot weather (1870) my headquarters for ten days had been established at Shimoga, in Western Mysore—a place in those days famous for big game of all sorts, from elephants downwards. Colonel Hay, the Deputy Commissioner, had not only placed his house at my disposal (he being out in the district), but had also arranged for immediate news being sent me of any tigers in the neighbourhood. Day after day kubbur (news) being brought in of kills, I proceeded to beat a series of most inviting looking nullahs, full of nooks, shaded by caroonda, jamun, and other evergreens, in the vicinity of the villages (Davidacoop and Moodinacoop) where the tigers had killed, but all in vain, for not a tiger was ever seen by anybody on these occasions.

One morning a bāil had actually been killed between rows of houses inside the village of Moodinacoop, and a few days later four were killed within half a mile of the same place. On two occasions we carried the pugs to the foot of a bare conical hill, about 150 feet high, which was crowned by a small Hindoo temple, about the size of a summer-house. Beyond the hill was flat, open country, devoid of covert, and we were completely foiled by this tiger. A fortnight after leaving Shimoga a friend wrote to me that, a native having seen the tiger enter the temple one morning, news of it was despatched to Shimoga, and Mr. Dobbs, a well-known sportsman in those parts, on proceeding there found a tigress and two cubs in possession of the shrine, and shot the lot without much difficulty.

Our march, on leaving Kowlass, lay through a maidan (flat country) for several days, where we had some sport with small game and antelope, and a day's rather unsuccessful pig sticking near a village named Rampoor, where a tribe of Brinjarries (gipsies*) brought their dogs to beat a thick send-bund, in which a sounder had taken refuge, but we could not induce them to face the open country, and only had a few short gallops, which were ended by the pigs regaining the covert. On reaching Bokur we had good sport with panthers and bears, some of the episodes of which have been already related. One morning news arrived of a gāra in the Soamtannah valley. Beaters having been sent for, we duly proceeded there, and were posted across a shady nullah, Manley on the left, Poulton on the bank of the nullah in the centre, and I on the right on some rising ground. In the first beat two tigers appeared; one went down the nullah towards Poulton, the other kept towards the left flank, heading straight for Manley's post. He, however, could not resist firing when the brute was some forty yards off, moving through some fairly open jungle, and missed him. The tiger then dashed towards the nullah, and passed under Poulton's tree, who fired both barrels, with similar result. Almost at the same instant the other tiger—which had approached unseen down the nullah—also passed under Poulton, who used his second rifle, but again without effect.

The first tiger then emerged from the nullah, about fifty yards behind Poulton, and I fired at him when he was some 120 yards off, and also missed him. Poulton saw this bullet strike the bank of the nullah, just over the back of tiger No. 2, within a few inches of it, and thought, of course, I had fired at him, but he was invisible from my

* Itinerant grain vendors.

post. A little less elevation might have resulted in stringing the pair! The next beat—a short one—was blank; we then had tiffin in the nullah, and each man endeavoured ineffectually to explain away his bad shooting, one and all vowing they would not let the next chance slip. The beaters were then sent by a circuituous route to the lower end of the valley to bring it back towards us. They were divided into three parties, a central one of about seventy men, and two wings of forty men each. Both tigers were again soon on foot, and made several attempts to break back through the beaters. One succeeded in doing so, but the other was gradually pushed forward to us, the beaters being admirably handled, and all attempts to turn their flanks being defeated by an advance of the threatened wing, the remainder of the line moving towards that flank in file. Eventually the brute was bowled over by Poulton as she lobbed past his post, the bullet striking her spine and paralysing her on the spot. We descended from our trees and approached her to within ten yards with the intention of going still closer, but she looked so fiendish, that discretion gained the day, and a bullet through the brain put her out of misery. She was 7¾ feet long and beautifully marked. Regardless of ticks we then proceeded to sit on the carcase and, to have a drink of triumph, but our united weight was too much for her interior economy, and a sepulchral rumbling was heard underneath us, when a most ridiculous stampede ensued. Rushing for our rifles, we fell head over heels, the natives swarmed up the trees, utter confusion prevailed for a few moments, but as the tigress remained unmoved the real state of affairs was soon recognised. Some of the beaters bolted to their village two miles distant, and gave out that the sahibs had all been eaten by a demon in tiger form, which pretended to be dead in order to seize them without trouble.

This led to subsequent difficulty in getting beaters. During the eight days we were at Bokur we also got thirteen bears and four panthers, and then proceeded to Pota in the Nandair district, meeting some pigs and bears there. We here made the acquaintance of Major Havelock, of the Nizam's Infantry, who had come from Hingolee to accomplish the death of a tiger that had killed his shikari under the following circumstances: They were beating one day near Golamorra, the shikari being utilised as a stop, with orders to fire at the tiger if necessary, and, as it attempted to break in his direction, he fired at and wounded it slightly. It then entered a thick patch of jungle, and Havelock, with the shikari, pushed on ahead to intercept it. The shikari was carrying a light ten foot bamboo ladder to enable his master to get up trees with facility. This he adjusted to a selected tree, and Havelock was in the act of mounting, the shikari holding the foot of the ladder, when he heard the growl of a tiger, and, looking round, beheld the unfortunate man in its clutches on the ground within a few feet of him. The rifles were also on the ground, and he was obliged to witness the tragedy that followed without being able to render any help. The poor fellow expired almost immediately, and Havelock, failing to find the tiger again, returned to cantonments. When we met him he was marching towards Golamorra with the intention of again searching for the tiger, but as we were the first on the ground, the choice of it lay with us according to the unwritten law of the jungle, and he was consequently obliged to entrust us with the mission of retribution.

We promised to let him know the result of our endeavours, and a fortnight afterwards, at Golamorra, news was brought into camp one morning, that a buffalo had been killed in a send-bund two miles distant, which was one of the tiger's favourite haunts. There was a large tank close by, where he was in the habit of drinking, the jungles all round abounded with nilghai, cheetul, sambur, and pig; but in spite of all this luxury, his reputation was an evil one, the natives alleging that, although not a professed man-eater, he varied his bill of fare about once a month with a human being, his last victim being a toddy man, who was killed and eaten in the very tope we were going to beat. His realms extended as far as Paradi, some ten miles off; the intervening country swarmed with game, especially nilghai and pig, so there was no excuse for his penchant for human flesh. Beaters having been procured with some difficulty, as it was a jungly district containing but a few small villages far apart, we proceeded to the tope, enlisting some Brinjarries as beaters on the way. The grove was partly composed of date palms, and partly of ordinary deciduous trees, such as mhowa, wood apple, kino, and ailanthus, all now denuded of foliage; with the exception of a mango tope at one end. From a distance it much resembled an ordinary English rectangular wood of six acres in extent. We were posted in echelon, Manley being on the left front, and I on the right in rear, some sixty yards behind Poulton. The tiger soon appeared, passing Manley at about thirty yards distance, and, on being fired at by him, he charged straight under Poulton, who also fired, causing him to swerve towards me. He came crashing along through the undergrowth of stunted palms, but I could not see him till he was almost underneath me, and then missed him clean. He pulled up within thirty yards, and trotted quietly towards me, eyeing me all the time, and evidently calculating the chances of being able to pull me off my perch. I could see all this performance by looking over my right shoulder, but could not stir to bring the rifle to bear on him, owing to my position on a branch. Coming to the conclusion I was out of his reach (at least sixteen feet above ground) he decamped, and we tracked him for a mile towards the Apparowpett nullah, about three miles off, but saw no more of him that day. The author of "Shikar Sketches" (Mr. Moray Brown) states that on a certain occasion he saw a tiger spring up a tree, leaving the marks of its claws about fourteen feet above the ground; it is therefore certain that nobody can be safe at a lower elevation, but in the Deccan one is seldom higher than twelve feet, as an idea prevails that a tiger cannot reach that height. I believe that without making any spring a tiger can reach nine feet; a glance at any tree which has been used by them for sharpening their claws will show seams in the bark that height, and a slight extra exertion should add several feet to it. A great friend of mine—a gallant officer of the 76th Regiment—met his death by being pulled out of a tree by a tiger, although he was posted some eighteen feet above the ground, the tree, however, was an exceptional one, being solitary and almost branchless, with a gnarled trunk covered with knobs, up which a tiger could easily climb; in fact, it much resembled a pollard willow. It happened near Tarcherla—a small village on the banks of the Godavery—in a district I had specially recommended him to try. The tiger—towards the end of a long beat—came down a rocky slope near the tree, which was in open ground near the foot of the slope, my friend and his shikari, being perched on the stump in a very conspicuous position. On being fired at the tiger charged towards them, and, leaping up, clawed the shikari to the ground, where he worried the unfortunate man for some time before an opening for another shot was given. Directly it was fired he ceased biting the shikari (who was dead) and, although hard hit, again sprang up the tree and dragged my poor friend to the ground. Here a desperate struggle was being fought when a brother officer came running up, but for some seconds he was unable to fire without hitting his companion, who was lying on the ground and pummelling the tiger about the head as it attacked him. He soon, however, got an opportunity, and shot the brute dead—but, alas! too late to save the life of his companion.* When posted in a tree, great difficulty is often experienced in aiming at an animal passing to the right—unless one can shoot from the left shoulder, an accomplishment well worth the trouble of learning. To some extent this may be guarded against by assuming a special position to bring fire on the right or left flank, as the case may be. The branches however may interfere with this; for instance, in the Golamorra wood I was standing on a branch that was almost horizontal, and to increase my stability was leaning forward against an almost similar one, a few feet higher and to the front. This position gave me command of all ground in front, but no fire could be brought to bear on an animal anywhere in rear, nor could I turn round to do so. Major Fergusson, of the Rifle Brigade, told me he got over this difficulty in the case of his first tiger, which suddenly appeared on his right rear, by holding on to a branch with his left hand, and using his rifle pistol fashion with

* Cases of panthers acting in this way occur from time to time, sometimes with fatal results; but it is a far more active animal than a tiger, and can climb like a cat.

A TRAGEDY.

THE GOLAMORRA MAN-EATER.

the right. In case of a very easy shot this might do, but the recoil of a 12-bore, burning five drachms, which I generally used, would be unpleasant, if not dangerous, under the circumstances.

The morning after the Golamorra fiasco we proceeded to beat the nullah towards which the tiger had been tracked at Apparowpett. The main nullah was deep and shady, and contained some pools of clear water at the bends ; beyond it lay two smaller watercourses, both were dry and ran parallel to the large nullah at intervals of about forty yards. The beaters commenced before we were posted, and we were hustled into our places, I being on the centre nullah some sixty yards forward, and Poulton and Manley to the right and left rear respectively on the flank nullahs. I had just got seated in my tree—a young and shady Indian beech—when a look-out man in a high tree behind me began to whistle at intervals, denoting that he saw the tiger. At the same instant I was attacked by red ants. In view of the approaching tiger it was inexpedient to descend, but the bites of the ants were maddening, and after a few agonising seconds I had to do so, remaining at the foot of the tree in its shade and carefully scanning the ground in front, which was covered here and there with patches of long yellow grass. The look-out man continued to whistle, and then pointed towards the big nullah; but for a long time nothing could be seen, until at length a movement about thirty yards to the left caught my eye, and there was the tiger walking slowly along nearly past my position. As the trigger was pressed he seemed to stumble in the dust, and then charged on without speaking in the direction of Manley, who gave him both barrels and sang out that he had gone on. The tracks were then followed up towards Manley's post. The brute had entered the nullah, and jumped a pool of water some eight feet in breadth. On seeing this it was clear that he was not hard hit, for if badly wounded he would probably have rushed through instead of jumping over, the stream. Manley also reported that he had not spoken to his shots, so we concluded he was missed, and, leaving directions for the beaters to use plenty of rockets, made a detour, and were again posted about half a mile ahead. Instead of ants my tree this time contained a nest of the small yellow tree bees, which are stingless, and I accordingly helped myself to their honey. This they resented by charging against my face and neck, causing much annoyance; to add to the discomfort the rockets discharged by the beaters had set fire to the long grass, and we were nearly stifled. Half blinded by the smoke, and grilled by the intense heat of sun and fire, I distinguished myself by firing at an imaginary tiger—a log of yellow wood striped with the shadows of the thick stems of coarse grass; this concluded the day's sport. Next morning the body of the tiger was found in some long grass behind Manley's tree. Our shots had all hit him, and any one of the lot would have been fatal. My shot, a shell, had entered behind the near shoulder and burst in the lungs; in spite of this he had jumped a nullah, received two more bullets; and covered 150 yards of ground before he collapsed. We also found the bullet which had been fired by Havelock's shikari—a very small one, which had only penetrated a few inches into the muscles of the shoulder. The tiger was one of the short-tailed breed and very powerfully built, with an immense skull, but the skin was completely destroyed by the firing of the long grass. While here, rumours reached us of a sahib having been killed by a tiger in the Mahoor country, some thirty miles to the north; but a few days later intelligence arrived that he was not dead, but had been badly mauled by a wounded tigress, which he was following up when the brute suddenly sprang out of a nullah and bit him severely. He (Captain Preston, of the Sherwood Foresters) providentially recovered, which very few do who have been in a tiger's clutches, the wounds, if not fatal on the spot, generally resulting in pyæmia. Wounds either by teeth or claws, should always be syringed with very dilute carbolic acid (one part acid to thirty of water), and cloths or lint saturated with the solution should then be applied to them. At a place named Makmudpully, we went out one evening to watch for bears at some caves on rising ground close to the camp. Poulton and I were first posted, the shikari then taking Manley off through the jungle to the far side of the ridge. Presently several shots in quick succession came from his direction, and imagining he had got into a scrape with some jānwars we ran to his assistance. On nearing his post we almost stumbled over a dead tiger which he had just shot. He explained that as they were ascending an adjacent small hill—the shikari Baliyah leading—a tiger jumped out within a yard of him from under a rock. He was carrying a 12-bore gun, loaded with ball, and the right barrel sent its projectile clean through the brute's heart at a range of five yards. She rolled over kicking, whereupon Baliyah, who was greatly excited, declared she was coming to life again, and urged Manley to keep on firing to the tune of six more shots, which, however, did not spoil the skin, the first shot being the one that did all that was required. She was a very handsome "royal," the stripes running round the body without a break. During the night two tigers were roaring—or "moaning" rather—round the camp within a few hundred yards. Our bed cots had been placed about a hundred yards off in an open space, in the moonlight, but these nocturnal noises were not conducive to sleep, so we had them shifted to safer quarters. The shikaries said these were two male tigers who had been paying their addresses to the tigress which had been shot. They would not kill our ties, so we beat for them on several occasions, but in vain.

This being Manley's first tiger we duly celebrated the event, the shikaries getting a goat for curry and extra arrack, while we drew on our stock of champagne, which was only broached on tiger killing days.

This jungle consisted of a series of small rocky hills full of caves and thickly covered with scrub jungle, not of the usual deciduous kind, which is always bare of foliage in the hot weather, but of evergreen shrubs—caroonda, jaman, bair, and the like—which would render it very difficult to see a tiger, while the features of the ground made it highly improbable that beating would be of any use. We therefore determined to sit up in case of a kill, which, as above stated, did not occur. Such procedure is allowable, and even advisable, in jungles akin to this, but it is poor sport even if the tiger appears, which he is most likely to do just about sunset. This plan may also be adopted in the case of a "chōr" (rogue) tiger, which has been in the habit of absconding after killing, and returning next evening to finish his repast. Tigers are undoubtedly fond of gamey flesh, and will sometimes lie near a kill until it is putrid. In the Annamullay Hills they revelled on the carcases of bison in this condition, and in the Mysore country the carcase of an elephant several days dead was a great delicacy to the genus *felis*—tiger or panther.

Apropos of sitting up, a very good story was going the rounds of the Madras Club some years ago, of a well known and popular lawyer who with two friends was out in the Mofussil (provincial districts) on a half pic-nic, half shikar trip. One day news arrived of an ox having been killed by a tiger in some adjacent jungle, which, owing to its extent and thickness, was unsuited to driving operations. They therefore decided to sit up over the gāra, and having sent coolies to erect a comfortable munchāl (platform) in a tree overhanging the kill, they ordered a substantial tiffin rather late in the afternoon, which it was intended should take the place of dinner, as they did not expect to return until the following morning. Repairing to the scene of the kill some time before sunset, they mounted the platform, which was luxuriously fitted with rezais (padded quilts). The tiffin had been sumptuous and the evening was sultry, and before an hour had elapsed they had all dropped off to sleep. In the middle of the night one of the trio fell overboard and commenced to groan with pain at the foot of the tree. This noise awoke his companions, who, believing it to be the tiger, promptly loosed off four barrels in the direction of the sound, but providentially missed hitting their companion.

CHAPTER VIII.

THE TIGER (*Felis tigris*).

My first tiger—Passes between the guns—Spur fowl indicates approach—Easy shot—Tracking up—Demoralised dogs—Find tiger dead—Its measurements—Hall wounds tiger—Mysteriously disappears—Difficulty of seeing—Meet two tigers—Patterson's pony—Scarcity of man-eaters—Benkipore man-eater—Kargeehully ravine—Beaters form groups—Hyena mistaken for tiger—Result—Large tiger at Benkipore—Swims river—Returns—Stampede—Shoot tigress at Komalapully — March to Rajavole — Joined by Colonel Russell—Gāra—Tiger escapes—Another gāra—Same result—Tiger's tactics—Two more gāras—Arrangements for beat—Tiger shot—Mankote—Penconda—Pakhāl lake—Variety of game—Chundraopett—Bobbery elephant—Tiger marked down—Charges—Death of the Romper—Tiger shooting not necessarily dangerous — Staunch elephants scarce—Shooting tigers on foot—Death of Doig—Devaroy Droog—Shoot a beater—His recovery—Sporting parties—Adventure with boar—Small rope useful.

After many days' unsuccessful beating in various jungles in the Deccan and Mysore (forty-seven days without even seeing a tiger), my first tiger was shot near Santawerry, on the Baba Booden Hills, in Mysore, in 1870. The previous fortnight had been devoted to a solitary and unsuccessful excursion so far as tigers were concerned—down to the plains, and on the morning of the 13th May I had ridden twenty miles from Kadoor, to join my friend Patterson on the hills. On arrival there, I found that all the sahibs (six) were beating for a tiger on a hill opposite the bungalow. My rifles had not yet arrived, but, taking a spare one of Patterson's, I went off to join them. They had been beating some time before my arrival, but without seeing anything. An hour later on, the tiger was startled by the beaters, and passed between the gun on my left and me. We never saw the brute, although we were only sixty yards apart, and in fairly open ground—nor would we believe it, until the pugs were pointed out. A few small patches of yellow grass—barely enough covert for a hare—were dotted about in the glade we were watching, and how the tiger passed through these without being seen is still a mystery, for we were both on the look-out, hearing the beaters shout "hūli" (tiger). The next beat was about half-over, when a spur-fowl started up with a note of alarm, some fifty yards in my front: this was soon followed by a slight rustling noise, as of some large animal walking with measured tread on the dead leaves in the undergrowth in front; it seemed to be moving from side to side, as if hesitating to emerge from the thicker covert. As the beaters approached, the "crinkle—crinkle" on the dead leaves became more distinct, and soon a handsome tiger appeared about thirty yards off, coming slowly down the thinly-wooded slope, straight towards my tree—an ailanthus. Its head was swinging from side to side as it advanced panting from the heat, and it presented such an enticing mark that I was obliged to avert my eyes to avoid the temptation to fire. It approached thus to within fifteen yards, and then stopped to listen to the beaters; this was the long-wished-for opportunity, and, aiming a little in front of the near shoulder, and rather high (as I was twelve feet above the ground) the trigger was pressed. The tiger gave a grunt, sprang into the air, and was then obscured for a few seconds by the smoke, which, as it cleared away, revealed a striped mass writhing and tearing up the ground, during which performance I missed handsomely with the left barrel, and the tiger, retiring slowly up the slope, soon disappeared in the bushes, while I shouted to the beaters to climb the trees. Descending from my tree, I went over to the gun on the left—an old hand at the game—and asked him to cover me with his rifle, while I pugged up the tiger, assuring him it was probably dead. He replied, "Not a step shall I stir out of this tree until something is known about the tiger." After some interval all the guns came up, and wisely declined to follow the wounded brute into heavy jungle—whereupon, like the headstrong young fool that I was, I proceeded to do so alone, and had gone a few yards on the track, when Edward Hall pluckily came forward, and volunteered to help me. The tracks were plain enough, being marked by much blood, and in several places the claws had been driven into the ground with force, sure sign of a severe wound.

It was ticklish work, owing to the dense jungle, and the dogs would not stir from our heels, although generally very game. At length they went forward a few yards—every hair bristling—over the slope, some twenty yards ahead, but had hardly disappeared, when back they came all of a heap, and barking in a terrible state of mind. Some four or five natives had followed us, and this was the signal for a general stampede, most laughable only for the dangerous state of affairs. Everybody thought the tiger was on us; the natives were up the trees in a twinkling; we who were in front jumped behind the trunk of a large forest tree within a yard of us, remaining at the "ready" for fully half a minute, but the foe did not appear. With much difficulty I then ascended an adjacent tree, in order to "crane" over the top of the slope, and saw the tiger lying on the ground, apparently dead, about fifteen yards off. A shot having no effect, I descended, and, preceded by volleys of stones, we advanced and found the brute quite dead. The spherical bullet had entered exactly at the spot aimed at, and, traversing the lungs, had come out just behind the off shoulder. It was a handsomely marked tigress, but, thinking the orthodox measurement too small (it was probably about 7ft. 9in.), it was not recorded in the diary; the skin is entered as being 9ft. 5in. long, and no doubt it was well stretched to give this; but then it was my first tiger. She had two old bullet wounds in the neck, which had passed clean through, but missed the spine. One day a Brinjarry (called "Lombāni" in Mysore) brought in news of three kills near a place named Attagherry, some three miles lower down the hills; we collected five guns, and some beaters with dogs, and found the tiger had killed at the upper end of a long shady nullah. Patterson was posted at the lower end in the nullah, the remaining four rifles being placed at intervals on both banks towards the gāra. Edward Hall, who was posted at the upper end, near the kill, fired at and wounded the tiger at the commencement of the beat; it then, without speaking to the shot, charged down the nullah, and mysteriously disappeared. I was posted at the lower end, within fifty yards of Patterson, in a sandal-wood tree, and when the beaters arrived got down out of my tree, and, was crossing through the nullah, when some of the dogs with me began to bark in a small clump of bushes between me and Patterson, who at once shouted out, "Get out of the nullah; the tiger is within a yard of you." I lost no time in climbing up the bank, the dogs continuing to bark in the harsh way they always do when on a tiger or panther. The covert was very sparse, but we could see nothing, although we beat every foot of it. Patterson then joined us, and pointed out the spot where he had seen the tiger when he shouted to me, but it had disappeared again immediately, and our subsequent beats were blank. There was but one spot where it could have got away unseen, viz., between my post, which was vacated, and Patterson's tree, as it was open ground elsewhere. In this instance there was every accessory favourable for an accident, a wounded tiger in a nullah among a lot of beaters. But why should I have remained in my post after the beaters had passed it? Such a thing is never done without special orders. It may be said that the beat ought to have been stopped when the tiger was wounded, but this was uncertain, as blood was not discovered till the beaters had arrived within fifty yards of the end of the beat; they were preceded by dogs, and the covert was thin. It is wonderful how a large animal like a tiger can conceal itself on ground where there is barely cover for a hare. As a rule, you will seldom see his outline when he is attempting to hide or escape unseen; there appears to be a movement in the general colour of the herbage or scrub jungle, but no outline is visible, merely an undefined mass of vitality, which vanishes when motion ceases; and the same thing occurs with every wild animal, great or small, from an elephant down to a woodcock. One evening at Yemadody, a famous place for spotted deer, about six miles from Santawerry, I had strolled out with a rifle into some scrub jungle near a tank fringed with forest trees, and was passing a clump of caroonda bushes, close to a large peepul, when, a low growl reaching my ears, I peeped through the bushes, and saw a tiger about twenty-five yards off, moving slowly through the trees towards the camp, not three hundred yards distant. Knowing he must turn to the left to reach the scrub jungle, I watched a small glade towards which he was heading, and where he would give a clear broadside shot when crossing. Just at that moment another growl emanated from a spot a few yards to my right, and there, within ten yards, was another tiger, slowly heading in the same direction as its comrade, but, owing to the bushes, and its being tail-on to me, I could not get a fair shot, so resumed watching the glade, but as neither appeared, after some seconds I followed as noiselessly as possible till the confines of the camp were reached, but never saw them again, and they undoubtedly crossed into the scrub jungle when I was following them up, as the tank barred the way on the right. I then told Patterson what had occurred, offering to go halves in any damage done if he would tie up his pony. This he declined to do with a good deal of warmth; we had no baits available, and my horse was too big a bait, so the incident closed. We beat for them throughout the following day, but without result. In those days the forests from Shimoga, by Luckwalli, on to the Baba Boodens, were prolific in big game of all kinds, except buffaloes, which are not as a rule found south of the Nerbudda river; and, although tigers were numerous, a man-eater was very seldom heard of, owing, no doubt, to the abundance of pigs and deer throughout that district. A few years before an exception had existed in the famous Benkipore man-eater—a tigress which was credited with having killed over 250 human beings. Her favourite stronghold was the Kargeehully ravine, a heavily wooded nullah of large extent, three miles distant from the travellers' bungalow at Benkipore. My haylas were tied up there, and after two days there was a kill, followed by a beat. The tracks showed it was a tigress with two cubs, but the jungle was very dense, full of caroonda and jamun bushes, and over one hundred yards broad in places, and it would have required 150 beaters at least to work it properly, whereas but sixty could be obtained; moreover, although the man-eater had been killed, her memory was still green, and they kept too close together, leaving strips of jungle unbeaten.

I once lost a fine tiger in the Hyderabad country owing to the beaters grouping themselves in this way. We were beating a broad and dry nullah, which was said to be the favourite lurking place of a local cattle-lifter. Early in the beat a hyena was started, and somebody mistaking it for a tiger, raised the cry "Pedda puli." This unsteadied the beaters a good deal, and they commenced to gather into groups, in spite of the shikaries' efforts to preserve an unbroken line. It was a fearfully hot day in the month of May. The shikari wanted me to climb a tree, but it was not the weather for that sort of amusement, and I took up a position on a sloping sheet of rock, close to a cave on a small island in the nullah, having placed some palas-kino leaves on the burning rock to sit upon, and poured water from the "chăgul" * over my head to keep it cool. Presently a fine tiger came slowly down the nullah towards me. At that time I had a stupid and fallacious theory that—in addition to other cat-like attributes—a tiger's sight was bad in bright sunshine, and I accordingly made no attempt to conceal myself (which might have been done, as he was over 200 yards distant, and frequently hidden by bushes),

* A leathern bag holding two quarts of drinking water, which is kept cool by evaporation.

"I TRIED TO STALK HIM."

merely remaining perfectly still, in the belief that he would not discover me. My second rifle lay on the rock beside me, as the gun-carrier had been sent away to lessen the chance of being seen. When about eighty yards off he stopped, and had a good stare at me. I remained perfectly still, but he had evidently spotted me. He then moved a yard or two to his right, and quietly lay down under the tree I was to have been posted in. The foresight was "swimming" owing to the intense heat, and as the distance was too great for a certain shot, I tried to stalk him, but he was too much on the alert, and kept raising his head from time to time to watch me. The beaters came on in an irregular line of groups, and the tiger, watching his opportunity, doubled back through the line between two groups, passing them within a few yards without being seen. One cannot blame the poor natives for acting thus, unarmed as they are, and, considering everything, they work well and pluckily as a rule, when properly handled by a sufficient number of armed shikaries distributed among them, which gives them greater confidence. The Benkipore folk had also been shaken by an amusing incident, which had occurred shortly before my visit. The village shikari was my informant, and stated that about two miles up the river Boodra—which flows past the travellers' bungalow—there was a very large tiger, the largest he ever saw—like a horse in size (!)—and that a certain sahib went out one day to beat for him over a kill. They beat right up to the bank of the river, where he was posted in a large tree, but saw no trace of the tiger. So the sahib descended, and he and the beaters were walking along the bank towards a fresh beat, when suddenly the tiger jumped up from some long grass in the bed of the river, and entering the water, which was about thirty yards broad, swam towards the opposite bank. When he was almost across the sahib opened fire, whereupon the brute turned about and commenced swimming back again. More shots were fired without result, and the tiger was soon near *terra firma* again. As the jungle was low scrub, containing no suitable trees for climbing, a stampede ensued, the tiger remaining master of the situation! My last regular trip after tigers was in the Singareny district, in the Nizam's Dominions, in the hot weather of 1881, the party consisting of my colonel, Colonel Russell, commanding 12th Lancers, and self. Colonel Russell, being detained by duty, did not join us until we had been a week in the jungle, and we were only able to devote some five weeks to the jungles which remained untried. Previous to the arrival of Colonel Russell we had got a tigress at Komalapully, a well-known tiger haunt near the Warrungul road, some ninety miles distant from Secunderabad. We had employed "Kistiah," a famous shikari who lived in that district, which was a good one for tigers, as large herds of cattle grazed there during the hot weather, and it was well provided with water and shady jungle. He was assisted by three shikaries of lesser note, but all were plucky, reliable, and hard-working men. We arrived in camp about nine o'clock one morning in the month of March, and while at breakfast news of a kill was brought in. About one mile distant was a very remarkable conical hill of basaltic rock, at the foot of which a net-work of shady nullahs radiated throughout a tract of scrub jungle, which, stretching away for some miles, joined another hilly area, also a noted tiger haunt. The gāra was close to a small pond at the edge of the jungle near the base of the hill, and we were posted so as to intercept the tiger if it attempted to break away through this wooded zone.

THE KOMALAPULLY TIGRESS.

The beat commenced close to the foot of the hill, towards which we faced. The Colonel was posted in a tree about seventy yards to my left, I being on a small rock commanding a nullah about twenty yards to my right. I soon heard the coughing roar of a tiger, which had been disturbed by the Colonel and his gun-bearer on their way to their post, but nothing appeared for some minutes, when the beat commenced with the usual preliminary burst of tom-toms, horns, shouting, rockets, and blank cartridge—a delicious, if discordant, overture, which always sends a thrill of pleasure through a sportsman. The tiger roared in response, and immediately afterwards, appearing on the edge of the jungle about forty yards to my left, galloped over a slope of sheet rock in front, and crossing the nullah, halted broadside towards me under a tree forty yards off on the opposite bank. I raised my rifle to aim, and the slight movement catching her eye, she turned her head to stare at me. A second later the trigger was pressed; up she went on her hind legs, and then charged me straight as an arrow, roaring as she came, but fell stone dead into the nullah, within twenty yards of my post, the Express bullet having taken her clean through the heart. A prettily-marked tigress exactly 7ft. 10in. between uprights. The shikaries reported that two of her cubs, about the size of big monkeys, had taken refuge in a cave at the base of the hill, but as they could not be bolted, they recommended us to wait for them after sunset, which we accordingly did, but ineffectually, nor was a beat next day more successful. We heard afterwards that they had been found half starved in the jungle, and killed by some native shikaries. This was the most luxurious day's tiger shooting I ever enjoyed, the whole thing taking place within a mile of camp, from which we were only one hour absent. Four days later we were joined by Colonel Russell on our march to Rajavole, where we arrived on the 29th March, after an uneventful fortnight, during which we had high winds and comparatively cool weather. The second day after our arrival a gāra was reported, and the tiger marked down in a small rocky hill about two miles from camp. This we proceeded to beat, and very shortly afterwards three bears were driven out and passed to my left towards the Colonel's posts. Then a tiger made his appearance, heading in the same direction, so I did not fire, but, much to my surprise, neither did they. I therefore came to the conclusion that he had doubled back before reaching their posts.

The beat ended without a shot being fired, and it then transpired that the tiger had passed within twenty yards of my colonel, who being in an awkward position in his tree, could not fire. Three days afterwards we were beating over another kill, at a small isolated cluster of boulders about three miles from camp. We were certainly posted too near the tiger's lair, and he must have detected us. He lay till the beaters were almost on the top of him, being evidently most reluctant to emerge from his retreat, which he eventually did at full gallop, straight under the colonel, who was posted in a leafy tree, which prevented his seeing the tiger. I got two snap-shots at him as he galloped through the jungle about seventy yards off. He spoke to the left barrel, but went on. We then tracked him for some distance—dangerous work, which should seldom be resorted to without an elephant—but there were no signs of blood, and to this day I don't know where he was hit, for we never saw him again. This tiger undoubtedly winded us, for we were posted up wind and within seventy yards of the cairn he was hiding in; and, although we were all at least ten feet above the ground, it gradually rose in front towards the cairn, so that, as a matter of fact, we were actually on the same level as the tiger himself. He very nearly succeeded in getting away on the left flank without being fired at. The only fault of the Secunderabad shikaries is their neglect to credit the tiger with the fine sense of smell he is undoubtedly possessed of. When the covert is of ordinary thickness and extent, a tiger, as a rule, appears noiselessly and suddenly, perhaps within ten yards of one's post; but it not unfrequently happens in jungles where the withered leaves abound and are large—like those of the bastard teak, for instance—that his approach is heralded by their rustling under his tread; but from small isolated hills or piles of rock where he has to cross the open ground, he bolts like a rabbit at full gallop, and usually gives a pretty difficult shot. In such spots, however, the space available for his escape, being limited, can generally be commanded by two rifles, and any extra ones should be utilised as "long stops," in case he gets through the first line.

A few days after the occurrence just recorded, news of two gāras was brought in, and that the tiger was "ringed" into the small hill, the scene of our first day's defeat. The monkeys had discovered, and were swearing at him, and as this annoyance might induce him to shift his quarters, we pushed on quickly to the ground. On the way we examined the carcases of the two haylas, which were within a few hundred yards of each other, and had been dragged into the shade of some bushes near at hand, to protect them from the vultures in accordance with a tiger's invariable custom.* Very little remained of either, but one had been killed by a tigress and cubs, which had gone

* The remains of one of these had been carefully covered up with leaves by the tiger.

away to some thick jungle which lay two kōss towards the east, and was beyond our sphere of operations that day. The second tiger was lying up close at hand in the small hill already described. Orders were issued to post the guns at a greater distance from the hill than heretofore, and the beaters were to commence further off from its base. The two colonels were in trees about fifty yards behind their former positions, I—acting as "long stop"—about seventy yards in rear. The tiger soon appeared, coming slowly down the face of the hill to within fifty yards of Colonel Russell, but a stop which had been placed in my original post, causing him to turn to the left, he presently emerged at a gallop between the two colonels, who fired simultaneously, and he rolled over and expired in a few seconds. He was a good average specimen of a short-tailed tiger, measuring as follows: Round fore-arm, 17¾ inches; length from nose to tail between uprights, 8 feet 2 inches; length of tail, 31½ inches.* We stayed two days longer at Rajavole without a kill, and then marched to Mankote, having a scuffle with bears on the way, which we found already in possession of a rocky hill we had intended to ambuscade at break of day. We encamped in a mango tope full of interesting birds, including several orioles and specimens of the white and chesnut paradise fly-catchers. Here, too, we laid in a supply of good drinking water, which was bottled off in view of possible contingencies elsewhere, the water in the district ahead being reported scarce and bad. Bears were numerous, and we had some fun with them, but, there being no news of tigers, we marched for the Pakhal Lake, by Penconda and Yellagooda, through a country affording bears and panthers,

* With a tail of ordinary length, he would have been more than nine feet long.

but no tigers that would kill, although at Gazelgut one of our coolies who was tying up a hayla was chased by a tiger and treed, the brute keeping watch over him for some hours.

We arrived at the lake on the 11th April and pitched our tents on the bund, a well-known camping ground, at the back of which lies a famous stretch of jungle, where we found tracks of tigers, panthers, bison, bears, nilghai, spotted deer, and pigs; but the tigers would not look at our ties, owing, no doubt, to the abundance of more toothsome food available. We had a few drives, and got shots at bears and cheetul; did a little bison tracking and boating (we had brought a canvas skiff, which was carried by two coolies from camp to camp), and after a few days marched to Chundraopett, having sent on shikaries to tie up coolgas.* The day previous Colonel Russell had to return to headquarters, his leave having expired. On our way to Chundraopett the shikari met us to report a kill in an adjacent nullah, which we accordingly beat, but found blank, Kistiah reporting that it was by a tigress and cub, and that the carcases of no less than four bāils were in the same nullah, which had all been killed within the last few days; but this jungle stretches as far as the lake, a distance of twelve miles, so it was a hopeless task to attempt to beat it, unless a tiger should have been ringed into a certain area. All this tract of jungle is now preserved by the Nizam for his own sport. The next morning there was a great commotion in camp, as one of the elephants, while collecting reeds for forage at a neighbouring pond, had lost his temper and knocked his keeper over with his trunk, and then knowing he had done wrong, had

* Another name for water buffaloes.

bolted away trumpeting to the jungle hard by. The man was a good deal knocked out of time and bruised, and his wife came to us in tears to say that the elephant would certainly kill him as it was a vicious brute, and had already dispatched three of its former keepers.

As she was speaking we could hear it trumpeting and tearing up trees in the jungle a short distance off, and as the mahouts said it was advisable not to attempt its recapture until it had cooled down a little, we returned to our tents. In a quarter of an hour there was an alarm that the brute was invading the camp, so we went out with our rifles, which of course were only to be used in case of absolute emergency.

The elephant stopped within twenty yards of the tents, and was eventually captured and shackled by the assistance of his comrade, and after a good deal of trouble. Meanwhile "Kistiah" had arrived with news of a tiger having been marked down in a small hill two miles distant, in a patch of scrub jungle which was in an isolated position, and that we were certain to get a shot at him, adding that he had been seen to approach one of our haylas, but, after a searching inspection, evidently came to the conclusion that it was not succulent enough, for he passed on and took up his quarters in the isolated hill aforesaid, where two coolies were left to watch him.

On account of the delay caused by the elephant's escapade we did not leave camp till ten o'clock a.m., and then took both elephants with us, the culprit's hind legs being loosely fettered, which caused him to shuffle along in a peculiar way, this being a preliminary part of his punishment, which the mahout said was to consist mainly of low dieting and stoppages of all elephantine luxuries, such as his daily allowances of jāgree (coarse sugar) and masala (spices) for at least one month; he also declared that the elephant, being an old offender, knew perfectly well what was in store for him, but that it would be wrong to use corporal punishment, which would only have the effect of making him more vicious. On arrival at the ground the Colonel was posted without difficulty, but for half an hour I failed to find a climbable tree. The sun was coming down like molten lead, and finally—in despair and exhausted by my efforts—I took up a position in a shady tree only a few feet above the ground, being unable to reach the higher branches. We could see the beaters arrive on the sky-line of the hill some three hundred yards distant, and conspicuous among them was my bāil wallah,* a tall fellow in a red turban, who had begged to be allowed to see the fun. He discharged the first rocket into a cave, which was immediately followed by the tiger charging him and Yelliah, one of the shikaries. They, however, both stood their ground like men—Yelliah blazing off his musket in the brute's face in concert with Kistiah and Ali, who also fired off their weapons (loaded with blank cartridge) in the same manner from an adjacent rock, amid deafening uproar from the beaters. After dashing about, and making ineffectual sallies at other points of the line, he charged down the hill towards the left flank, but, being headed by the stops, came straight towards me after making an ineffectual spring at the last of the stops, who was posted in a tree some fifty yards to my left front. I then lost sight of him for a few seconds; he almost immediately emerged at a slower pace, but the raising of my rifle caught his eye, and, with a

* Bullock man.

few coughing roars, he turned on full steam again, and came at me. On firing the right barrel the smoke hung, so I kept the rifle to my shoulder ready to pull again in case of pressure at the muzzle, but in a couple of seconds was much relieved by seeing my antagonist quivering on the ground within twelve yards. The Express bullet, entering just over the left eye, had brained him; half an inch higher it would have been a clean miss. This was the last tiger I shot, a fine sporting brute. We christened him "the Romper." The defaulting elephant was detailed to carry the body back to camp, as another instalment of punishment, to which he at first objected very strongly, but finally succumbed to his fate. Tiger shooting is not nearly so dangerous a sport as many people imagine; a certain element of risk is inseparable from it as from many other sports, but it adds to the excitement.

Shooting from a howdah is undoubtedly the safest way of killing tigers, always provided that the elephant is staunch, and will not bolt. If there are trees about, it then becomes extremely dangerous, as the occupants as well as the howdah, run a good chance of being smashed up. We were unlucky as a rule with the Hyderabad elephants, only three of which had the reputation of being reliable. In my earlier days of tiger shooting I had undergone this ordeal, and as a friend had the stock of his rifle smashed while attempting to guard off a bough, we then and there declared that we should never again try tiger shooting from an elephant, unless it was certified as being staunch. The mahouts cannot be believed, as they always swear by their particular animals, as a sailor does of his ship. It is a great mistake to remain on the ground, if there is a rock or tree near you. A tiger may be shot through the

MY LAST TIGER.

heart, and still be able to kill you before he dies. Anything is better than being on the ground; an elevation of four or five feet will at all events give you the advantage of increased command of ground. If posted on the ground, don't fire at a tiger above you, *i.e.*, on higher ground, unless he is moving laterally, and clear of you. He will always bound forward in prolongation of the line of his body when struck by a bullet, and not knocked over or killed dead. Don't fire at him when you are on the ground. If he is approaching in your direction, let him pass, and take him as he goes away —he will on being hit spring forward in that direction; if, however, he is coming straight towards you, there are three alternatives — (1) show yourself, and he will probably swerve off, offering you a fairly safe shot, or it may head him to another gun, but don't wait until he is too close, as all such animals, when suddenly encountered, are liable to become aggressive; or tap a tree or rock without showing yourself, and he will alter his course, probably giving you or one of your companions a favourable shot; or, if he is halted, offering a very easy shot, he may be brained by a cool hand, who is clear of his death-spring—but this is a dangerous alternative, and cannot be recommended. As he walks through a jungle, the tiger does not look up above his own level—consequently, if properly posted, he will not see you. His senses of sight and smell are very keen; these facts are frequently forgotten. A "cumbley" (blanket) or other article, if hung upon a bush, will generally head a tiger from that point, and save a "stop."

Following up a wounded tiger is dangerous work when no staunch elephant is available; but in fairly open jungle, with at least three rifles—*i.e.*, two men in addition to yourself—it may, as a rule, be attempted. A native climbs a tree to scan the ground in front, and the guns advance slowly shoulder to shoulder, rifles at full-cock, the centre gun watching the front, and the others their respective flanks. On gaining thirty yards or so a fresh tree is ascended, and a further forward movement made. If a tracker is necessary, he should be armed himself, and must work under the muzzles of the sportsmen's rifles. It is not fair to expect a man to undertake such work unarmed, and there are many instances on record where shikaries have done good service with their weapons at such close quarters. If the jungle is very thick, it may be set on fire if it will burn, but no advance can be made on foot with safety; the recent sad death of Colonel Hutchinson in the Belgaum district, exemplifies the danger of such an attempt.

A solitary sportsman should never follow a wounded tiger into covert on foot, for he cannot do the work of three men—*i.e.*, keep watch to front and flanks. Two of my acquaintances have met with their deaths by doing so. The first (Captain Doig), in 1868, followed a wounded tigress into some scrub jungle near Trimulgherry, and carried the tracks into a nullah fringed with custard apple bushes, which do not afford much covert in the hot weather, being then bare of foliage. While examining the tracks, the tiger appeared suddenly on the left flank, and killed him—to the best of my recollection—before he could again fire his rifle.* In any case, where covert is thick, the betting is entirely in the tiger's favour; he can see without being seen, can select his opportunity, and

* The last case was that of the late Lieutenant-General the Honourable Sir J. Dormer, Commander-in-Chief, Madras, who followed a wounded tiger into a sholah, and received wounds from which he died.

probably land among the sportsmen before a shot can be fired.

In October, 1881, I had for several days been beating the jungles at Devaroydroog, near Bangalore, for a tiger which was killing a lot of cattle in the vicinity, but without seeing anything of him. A fair number of cheetul and pig, and a few sambur, had been driven out daily; but, being keen about the tiger, I had not fired a shot. The beaters and camp followers were very clamorous for meat; but I told them that on the last day of my leave the village shikaries would help, and that we would have a big beat for deer and pig, and get them plenty of meat.

Accordingly, on the evening of the 20th October, I moved down the hill to Kombarhully bungalow, which was situated close to a thickly wooded tract of hitherto undisturbed jungle, which was to be the scene of our operations next day. About one hundred villagers, headed by four matchlock shikaries, having mustered at the bungalow at an early hour the following morning, we first proceeded to beat a shady valley, about half a mile in length, and three hundred yards broad, the beaters being formed into line, with a shikari on each flank, and the two remaining matchlock men three hundred yards in advance, with orders to move gradually forward on their respective alignments, to the top of the valley, where I was to be posted in a central position.

Towards the end of the beat my shikari said "there is a pig—fire," pointing to a moving object, under some bushes, about eighty yards distant. It was very indistinct, but, on pressing the trigger it emitted some grunts, and appeared to be rolling on the ground; reloading, I ran forward, and was just going to put another bullet into it when a man's arm projected from the struggling mass! It was one of the matchlock wallahs, who, trying to do a bit of shikar on his own hook, had crept forward from his flank position, receiving an Express bullet, which tore away the left side of his neck, from the jaw to the shoulder, but luckily missed the jugular vein. We made a litter of boughs and sent him to Toomkoor, to the native hospital, whence I received frequent reports that he was getting on well, the last of which, at the end of three weeks, was accompanied by a lawyer's letter, threatening me with dire penalties if a handsome sum was not forthwith forwarded as compensation. This letter probably cost the poor fellow a considerable portion of the sum remitted to him. The beat of the tiger we had been looking for, extended as far south as Magadi—another "droog" or hill-fort lying to the west of Bangalore—where periodical trips, under the management of a sporting "vet." took place on kubbar being received of its depredations. On one of these occasions the guns were duly posted, and, my friend being bored by a long wait for the beat to commence, descended from his tree and entered into conversation with an adjacent gun. Presently the preliminary din of tom-toms, &c., rose upon the air, announcing that the beaters had begun to work; but the sportsman declined to go back to his post, merely remarking "the tiger never shows up, he's a mythical brute," and continued to converse; when suddenly shouts of "bagh, bagh," caused him to bolt for his tree, against which a short bamboo ladder was leaning. The tiger charged right under him as he was ascending it, but, holding his rifle pistol-fashion in one hand, he loosed it off; the recoil knocked him off the ladder, and he fell heavily to the ground, while the tiger, untouched, but roaring loudly, disappeared into the jungle, and was not

KISTIAH AND HIS STAFF.

again seen. This gallant officer was the hero of a well-authenticated pig-sticking episode near Kamptee. The hunt shikari, in attempting to dislodge a boar from some thick covert, had been attacked and ripped; he cried out for help, and Mr. G. dismounted and entered the covert, but was immediately charged and knocked over by the boar, his spear being sent flying. He, however, managed to cling on to the boar's back, and actually rode him, till the rest of the party, having also dismounted, entered the covert and speared the brute. In addition to the light bamboo or rope ladder usually carried to facilitate the ascent of trees, for a tiger beat a small hempen rope, about fifteen feet long, will be found to be most useful for securing oneself, by loose lashing, to adjacent boughs when the desired height has been gained; a much freer use of the rifle will then be possible, and there will be little, if any, danger of an involuntary fall. We often extemporised a sort of chair, by passing this rope several times from one branch to another, the ends being firmly knotted, but when the sportsman takes up his position the surrounding circumstances will suggest many uses for this article, which should always form part of a tiger shooter's equipment. A shikar knife is an inconvenient and useless thing to carry as a rule, but when posted in leafy trees is occasionally necessary to lop off small branches that may interfere with the aim or view. Even when one is posted in a tree, and therefore practically safe, a thrill of pleasurable excitement will be experienced when a tiger is seen to be approaching in a direction that renders getting a shot a certainty. On such occasions, when a young hand, I used to avert my eyes and count ten seconds at intervals, to enable me to resist the temptation of firing before he had arrived within twenty yards.

CHAPTER IX.

THE INDIAN BISON (*Gavæus gaurus*).

A King of Beeves—Habitat — Measurements of—Danger of stalking solitary bulls—Bison on the Baba Boodens—Stalking in open—Trip to Annamullays—Virgin forest—Toonacudavoo Carders—Their chiefs—Mulsers—Plan of operations—Poolakul — Nocturnal noises—Tracking—Diffidence of Carders—Strike a trail—Fire a snap-shot—Wounded bison—Heavy rain — Shoot muntjack deer — Leeches — Aggressive monkey — Wound bull — He charges and is killed—Fresh tracks—Wound and kill another bison—Am nearly brained by a monkey—Bison meat—Flowering of bamboo—Famine—Tiger visits us.

According to naturalists, this animal is not a true bison, his ribs being too few, and his horns being differently shaped, to those of that species. They also say he ought to be called a "gaur;" however, as he is always known as a bison among Indian sportsmen, it will be convenient to adhere to that term. He is a veritable king of beeves, being larger than any other type of the bovine race, and some sportsmen assert that they have shot them up to twenty-two hands in height, but these measurements were probably taken along the curves—and the average height of a good bull is about eighteen and a half hands.

This magnificent animal inhabits the same type of jungle as the elephant in Southern India, and, broadly speaking, may be said to exist in all primeval forest lands, south of the River Nerbadda, such as the Travancore, Annamallays, and Palney Hills, Wynaad, Coorg, and Canara Forests, thence eastward through Southern Mysore to Denkanicotta, the jungles fringing the Western Ghauts as far north as Saugor, and those along the Eastern Ghauts, and their prolongation to the Sumbulpore forests, all harbour the bison. I have tracked them in the Mahoor and Pakhal districts of the Nizam's dominions, and since his Highness has taken a large tract of the country into preservation, they may be expected to increase and multiply accordingly. A few were to be found some years ago in that uninviting looking scrub jungle lying to the south-west of Cuddapah, but the cream of the bison country may be said to be in the triangle Bangalore, Mangalore, Travancore. The bull is from eighteen to twenty hands high, dark chocolate colour, with white stockings; length of horns, thirty inches; spread, thirty-eight, tip to tip, twenty-seven; length of head, twenty-two inches; the eyes are blue. These are the measurements of a good bull's head and horns, but I have records of two animals considerably larger.*

The cows are lighter in colour, and smaller in size, but in thick covert are easily mistaken for a bull; the height and horns of a good cow often approaching those of the male in size. In every point, it is a far superior animal to its American namesake, nor does it resemble that animal in any way, being probably at least twice its weight, and proportionately superior in size. It bears the reputation of being a more formidable animal than either tiger or elephant, and more dangerous to stalk, and among my acquaintances who have followed this sport several have been roughly handled, among others the late General Douglas Hamilton, of the Madras Army, a famous sportsman, Captains Barnett, Chamberlayne, and Gaisford, the

* *Vide* Chapter XV.

Carder Shikari Atlay, and others whose names I cannot just now recall; on all these occasions the bison had been wounded first. A case certainly occurred some years ago of an officer being attacked without provocation, and, to the best of my recollection, killed by a solitary bull, on the Western Ghauts, in the Bombay Presidency; but this must be considered exceptional, although on some occasions, I am bound to admit, that if the initiative had not been taken by me, the bison would probably have done so. These solitary bulls have always an evil reputation, resembling rogue elephants and buffaloes in this respect, but so far as my small experience goes, of something over forty skirmishes, with the herd—and some solitary bison—I have never been charged by an unwounded one, except on a certain occasion, when a herd led by a wounded bull came at me *en masse*, of which particulars will be given later on.

The first bison ever seen by me were in the Baba Booden Hills in 1870. This range is in Western Mysore, nearly semi-circular in shape, and up to 6000 feet high. It is isolated, and surrounded by heavy jungles containing all the varieties of Southern Indian big game, but, like all forests in these latitudes, very unhealthy. Higher up the slopes the climate is salubrious and delightful. On the above occasion we were going to drive a large sholah (wood) for Sambur; but before the guns were posted, a herd of about a dozen bison broke away on the far side and made off down the hill towards the low country forests. On this day, too, I saw a flying squirrel and a woodcock, a decidedly rare bird in India, although they are to be found on the Neilgherry Hills, and I remember three being shot in Burmah, near the Royal Lake at Rangoon, by a soldier in my regiment in the year 1876. A friend of mine—Mr.

Porter, who owned a coffee plantation, and was a good and experienced sportsman—used to declare that he knew of no better sport than bison-stalking on these hills—on the wide grassy plateaux near Kulhutty—herds of bison, being attracted by the young grass which springs up after the first shower of the monsoon, leaving their fastnesses in the jungles of the low country, came up to graze on these swards in the early mornings, retiring to the shade and streams of the sholahs when the sun got hot. Porter lived at Santawerry, five miles down the ghaut, and in order to be on the ground at dawn, was in the habit of coming up the hill the evening before to sleep in a cave adjacent to the favourite feeding grounds. These stalks in the open necessitated much greater care than those in the woodlands ordinarily frequented by bison, inasmuch as the sight of the animals had to be considered, as well as their keen sense of smell; nor were there any trees to protect him in case of a charge. My bison shooting, however, was almost invariably confined to the forest, my first trip being made in 1871 to the Annamullay Hills, and subsequent ones to Bandipore, Mudnoor, and the Chamraj-nugger jungles. The preceding three months of the hot weather in that year had been devoted to the pursuit of bears, panthers, and tigers, in various jungles lying between Hyderabad and Chanda, and on the commencement of the rains, I returned to Secunderabad, dawked to Gulbergha (it was before the days of the Hyderabad Railway), thence to Bangalore by rail; here laying in a fresh stock of provisions, ammunition, and equipment, the journey was continued by rail to Coimbatore, thence by road to Polachy, where everybody was down with fever, and I finally reached the village of Annamullay, at the foot of the hills, on the 27th June.

My sport commenced here, for the place was full of rats, which kept me going the whole night, resulting in five being slain. Next day a journey of fourteen miles up the ghaut road—which was almost impassable in places—landed me at Toonacudavoo, the headquarters of the Government Timber Department, the last ten miles of the march having been made through magnificent primeval forest, studded with peaks several thousand feet high. At intervals we passed clearings, where the places of the teak trees which had been felled and carted off, were taken by a younger growth, planted by the Forest Department, and which, although only a few years old, were already over twenty feet high. In addition to the teak, many other valuable timber trees flourished all round, the rosewood and blackwood being particularly noticeable. The bamboo was plentiful, and in many places the undergrowth of cannæ, caladium, elephant and lemon grass, was several feet high, although the rains had only commenced three weeks before. The change from the dazzling Deccan furnace to these fresh, green, cool heights was delightful.

At Toonacudavoo I was most hospitably received by Mr. Douglas, head of the Woods and Forest Department, who housed me in his comfortable bungalow, while supplies were being collected, and shikaries and coolies gathered from their jungle villages. The shikaries were all of the Carder tribe, and were headed by their chiefs or "moopens," of which there were two—Vyapoori and Atlay—both bearing scars of the chase, the former having lost an arm when elephant shooting, and the latter having been gored through the thigh by a bison which he incautiously approached believing it to be dead. When with me he used to take very good care that the accident would not recur, for when a bison was knocked over he never advanced till the body had been bombarded with sticks and stones for several minutes.

The coolies were supplied from the Mulsers, also a jungle tribe, who inhabited the lower slopes of the hills and were looked down upon—morally and literally—by the Carders. My plan of operations was to use Toonacudavoo as a strategic base from which expeditions could be made to certain hunting grounds within a radius of fifteen miles, supplies being obtained from it every third day. In order to keep the stores at this base up to the requirements, Douglas very kindly arranged to send coolies once a week to the village of Annamullay for rice, fowls, curry stuff, kids, arrack, and tobacco. This system worked admirably. A large tract of country was opened up for shikar, and the Carders and Mulsers ate and drank to their hearts' content. They chew tobacco, but will not smoke, believing it affects the lungs.

All being in readiness we started on the 30th June for Poolakul, seven miles to the south. Two Mulsers carried my tent, an old regulation single poler, with a double fly; two more carried camp utensils, groceries, and bedding; the remainder being Carders, and above this sort of work, carried my rifles and ammunition and their own food supply. My butler was left at Toonacudavoo as "master of the depôt;" but the "chokra" accompanied me, and we both carried a share of our own eatables—rice and fowls. He was a plucky boy of about fifteen years of age, and had been in the habit of carrying my second rifle and loading it for me during the previous hot weather.* My

* He never attempted to bolt, but in ticklish moments he used to carry the spare rifle in one hand, and hold on to my coat with the other.

camp was situated at the foot of a rocky slope, above which rose a high and wooded ridge, and magnificent forests stretched away on every side. The Mulsers, in an incredibly short time, rigged up a bamboo bedstead in the tent, and made a capital hut for the chokra to cook in. They then cut down some female bamboos and made water-buckets from the joints, and constructed reservoirs from the larger stems to hold our drinking and cooking water. During the night I heard the croaking of spotted deer, the bark of a muntjack deer, and the belling of a sambur on the slope above the camp, and many other jungle voices which I did not recognise. These sounds always augur well for sport. Next morning we started at daybreak up the slope above the camp, and, entering the wooded part, followed a bison track up the hill until the top was reached, a stiff pull of over a mile. Here we found ourselves on a thickly wooded plateau, the surface of the ground being covered with creepers and cannæ. In Indian file we followed an old bison path,* the tracker in front and the gun carrier behind me. The tracker, having the most important duty to perform, did not carry a rifle, and from time to time he changed places with his companion, who then took up the post of honour.

After walking in this way for some miles we struck the fresh trail of a bison, but the Carders' reputation as trackers was far in advance of their performance, which was only moderate; they seemed to track in a perfunctory way, as if they were bored; and on subsequent occasions I often longed for Baliyah, or Pochello; or some other of the keen shikaries of the Deccan. As Carders will not even touch a bison it may have had something to do with their

* These game-paths exist in all dense jungles.

diffidence. They soon came to a check, and, after ten minutes' search, asked me to help them, probably to test me. I made a wide cast outside the ground they had been over, and hit it off; this had a good effect. The art of tracking has always been most fascinating to me from the time I was twelve years old, and accompanied the keeper on his daily rounds when home for the holidays. At length, after two hours tracking, a cow bison, suddenly starting up in front, dashed away over a nullah full of long grass, at the opposite side of which a thick bamboo jungle hid everything from view, but we could hear the rest of the herd moving about in it some fifty yards ahead. Presently Atlay motioned to me to kneel down, as he pointed to a clump of bamboos in front. In vain I looked; nothing was to be seen but foliage; immediately afterwards a huge bull appeared for a second, round the edge of the clump, but before I could get the sights on him he snorted loudly, turned about, and crashed off through the thicket, followed by the rest of the herd. The noise they made as they dashed away through the jungle was prodigious, something like a cavalry charge, accompanied by a succession of rifle shots, caused by the breaking of bamboos. We followed the tracks for a mile before sighting them again, in the same class of jungle—bamboos—through which we could only get fleeting glimpses as they moved about between the clumps. Another hour passed in this way, when, my patience being exhausted, I took a snap shot at one; this was followed by another stampede of the herd, which thundered off through the forest in the usual way. I heard my shot tell, and in a short time, when following them up, we came to a spot where the wounded one had evidently halted, the ground being covered with blood; from here the tracks led into a patch of tangled creepers,* about four feet high and fifty yards across; we here proceeded with great caution, expecting to come on the brute every moment, as the tracks of blood were plentiful, but it had passed through and gone on.

On emerging into more open forest Atlay pointed out a bison standing about eighty yards off—end on—tail towards us. Believing this to be the wounded animal, I foolishly fired at it in this position, but the bullet only acted as an incentive to further flight. We then followed the tracks for nearly a mile, but, seeing no traces of blood, I inquired of Atlay if it was the wounded bison first fired at. He replied in the negative, so, retracing our steps to the patch of creepers, we soon recovered the lost trail, which we followed for several miles, only once hearing the bison stampede on our approach. The shikaries expected that it would have laid down from weakness within a mile or two of the spot it had first stopped at, but here it was, going away as fresh as paint, although still losing blood. At this juncture down came the rain in torrents, and soon obliterated the tracks. Further pursuit was hopeless, so we struck for the camp, shooting a muntjack deer on the way, which was lying under a fallen branch some sixty yards off. Although unsuccessful, it was a new phase of sport, and the day was enjoyable, the surroundings being so completely different to anything before experienced. Sometimes half an hour would be spent in comparative darkness, owing to the dense canopy of foliage, through which the light penetrated with difficulty, then we would suddenly emerge into a pretty glade bathed in sunshine, with, perhaps, a burn trickling down the centre, fringed with feathery bamboos

* Bauhinia—very common in these jungles.

and tree ferns, while clumps of flowering cannæ and lilies* studded the adjacent ground. In some of the little dells were to be found several kinds of ferns, chiefly varieties of maiden-hair and polypodium, but it was in an enchanting spot of this kind that I first encountered the hill-leech, a diminutive but repulsive reptile, which progresses by doubling up its body like a loop, and then projecting the head forward for another stride. I sat down to smoke a pipe, and soon discovered some of these pests skirmishing up my gaiters, and on pulling off my socks on arrival in camp, two hideous writhing objects rolled out on the floor of the tent. These little leeches are the curse of these and many other jungles. It is very difficult to keep them out, the best plan being to wear two pair of socks over the shooting breeches. If one pair of socks only is worn, they push their heads through, and, leaving the bodies outside, fill them from within. The bites are very irritating and liable to fester if scratched. Some parts of the jungles simply swarm with them, and elephants and bison give these places a wide berth.

On return to camp we found the chokra in a great state of mind, as, shortly after our departure in the morning, he had been interviewed by a very large "plenty bad" black monkey, which suddenly appeared at the door of his hut, and on his attempting to drive it away by throwing sticks and shouting, it made hideous grimaces and hostile demonstrations, pretending to jump on him. He said it would certainly return in the morning with its family to eat him, and that he could not stay alone in the camp another day, so a Mulser was left to keep him company. We started the following morning in a southerly direction, and walked for several hours, finding nothing but some elephant tracks

* Caladium.

three days old. For five long hours we toiled over hill and dale, through swamps and acres of tangled creepers, and were in the act of wading a nullah, when a herd of bison unexpectedly crashed up a jungle-covered hill in front. We followed, and soon saw a fine bull standing on the side of a hill about 130 yards ahead. Being new to the work, I fired. It is a mistake to do so at such comparatively long ranges. The bullet, however, struck him rather low. He ran a few yards and halted, not knowing whence the report came, and looking all round in a perplexed manner. I fired again, and heard the "squelch" of the bullet striking him, whereupon he ran straight towards us, and entered a patch of high creepers within fifty yards. Cautiously advancing, we followed up his tracks by making a detour, and entered the creepers very carefully, peering through the foliage, and momentarily expecting a charge. We soon discovered him lying down, but the dense covert gave no chance of a vital shot, and suddenly jumping up he rushed off, but he was too sick to go far, and we soon espied him about a hundred yards ahead, and, running up, put a bullet rather high through the shoulder. This provoked a charge, but he was too much knocked out of time to be very formidable, and a bullet through the brain ended the encounter. He was a fine bull nearly eighteen hands high, with fairly good horns, but being my first bison I thought him a splendid animal, and, sitting down on him, smoked the pipe of triumph. The herd having had time to settle down, we recommenced tracking, and again came upon them in a glade a quarter of a mile farther on, but they were much on the alert, bolting before another bull could be picked out, although some cows offered tempting shots, which were declined. The rain was coming down in sheets, and being thoroughly drenched, we returned to camp, where we found everything in a similar plight, as the tent was not waterproof. This being a successful day, all hands received a double allowance of arrack and tobacco, and were promised a kid for curry on return to civilisation.* On these occasions they invariably over-ate themselves, and were unfit for work the following day,† but having been once started, the custom could not be discontinued without offending them, as they—in common with all jungle wallahs—are particularly touchy and sensitive. It rained heavily and steadily throughout the night, but cleared for an hour about 5 a.m. next day, when, dispatching Mulsers for the head and marrow-bones of yesterday's bull, we started eastwards, up the rocky slope aforementioned, which I nick-named "Desperation Hill."

When we arrived at the top, the rain again descended in torrents, and kept steadily at it throughout the day, all the nullahs were in spate, and we had much difficulty in crossing the larger ones, once being very nearly swept away by the torrent. For six long hours we toiled through the forest, before sighting a fresh bison track, and even then the hoof marks seemed rather stale, being dulled by the rain.

After half an hour's difficult tracking up a very steep hill, covered with clumps of bamboo, we arrived at a spot where the herd had bolted on hearing us approach, this was plainly shown by the tracks, although we had not heard them, owing to the roaring of a torrent close by, and the

* The Carders are above serving for money—all they will take for their work being food, tobacco, and liquor.

† Not so much from the effects of arrack—of which they never got more than two glasses—as from over-eating.

noise made by the rain on the trees. We plodded on for another hour in pursuit, and were just crossing a waterfall when the body of a huge bison appeared near the top of a hill we were about to ascend, and some eighty yards off. It loomed so large in the mist against the skyline, that both the Carders exclaimed "anī" (elephant), but immediately afterwards we saw the horns, and, aiming for the heart, I fired.

The remainder of the herd crashed away, but the wounded one did not go far, stopping at the foot of the hill in the stream, among some thick bushes. Here Atlay could see the bison, but I failed to do so, and we were obliged to make a detour for a clearer shot. In the meanwhile the bison sloped off, up the opposite hill, which was crowned by crags and thick jungle. Here we proceeded with the greatest caution, peering into every bush before advancing. Atlay was well up to this game, and this was lucky, for the bison, having rounded the corner of a rock, lay in ambuscade in some thick bushes, awaiting us; but, on arriving at this rock, round which the tracks ran, Atlay took me over it, and pointed out the brute within five yards, head down ready to charge, as she had heard us approaching.

A bullet in the brain saved further trouble; it was a large cow, nearly seventeen hands high, with remarkably fine horns. We then followed up the tracks of the herd for about two miles, but as we neared them, they were alarmed by the hooting of some black monkeys, which were exceedingly hostile and demonstrative, and a stampede occurred. Shortly afterwards, one of the monkeys displaced a large rotten branch, which caught me on the helmet, and knocked me over unconscious. Being too much bewildered by the blow to aim correctly,

"HEAD DOWN, READY TO CHARGE."

the rascal escaped with a whole skin. and I returned to camp discomfited.

The marrow bones were cooked for my dinner, likewise the tongue, but the "esprit de bison," which pervaded them, was too much for my palate, nor could I ever afterwards look at bison flesh in any form.

In addition to the usual forest trees of the Annamullays, the bamboo was very plentiful in the vicinity of Poolakul. They were all female trees of the largest kind and luxuriant growth, being quite equal in every respect to those in Burmah. Owing to their prevalence the Carders declared that the best feeding grounds for elephants and bison lay here; but I had better sport with the beeves in the districts farther north, which, however, swarmed with leeches, while here they were comparatively scarce, the precincts of the camp being quite clear of these pests, which decline to cross over rocks or stones. The bamboos were at their best, as they were about to seed—a phenomenon that only occurs about once in a quarter of a century—immediately after flowering the seed is formed and shed; it resembles rice, and is equally prized as food by the natives; the tree then dies. A few bamboos flower and die every year; but an epidemic like this, extending over a large tract of country, is rare, and is said by the natives to be a precursor of sickness and famine—a prediction which in this case was soon verified.*

A tiger prowled round the camp every night, but the Carders did not mind him, and continued to sleep under a frail lean-to, made of plantain leaves and supported by sticks, three sides of which were open to the incursions of any nocturnal marauder; but one night they were very

* The great famine of Madras commenced the following year.

uneasy, when a herd of elephants came crashing through the adjacent jungle, declaring that whenever they saw huts they invariably pulled them down, and that my white tent would inevitably attract them. My friend Douglas told me that for several years the bungalow at Toonacudavoo had been regularly wrecked by these animals, probably out of pure mischief or curiosity.

CHECKING A CHARGE.

CHAPTER X.

THE BISON (*Gavæus gaurus*).

Is a hill animal—Bison fly—Smell of bison—Return to Toonacudavoo—Good sport—Lose several wounded—Walk into a herd—Wounded bull—Saturnalia in camp—Shoot a bison—Our guide loses the way—Night in the Currian Sholah—Wild dogs—Carders arrive—Fire at bull—Kill him—Bullet strikes horn—Another day in Currian Sholah—Wound a bull—Am charged by herd—A useful shot—Knock over another bull—First bull dies—Perrincudavoo—Shoot two bison—Elephant tracking—Shoot cow bison—Wound big bull—Tiger kills him—Shoot another bull—On short commons—Curried monkey—Mahseer—Return to Toonacudavoo—Poolakul again—Charged by cow—Fire at bogus bison — Leave the Annamullays — Trip to Wynaad — Bandipore—Prevalence of fever—Shoot large bull—Salt licks—Shooting herd bison—Big bores necessary.

Although often found in low-lying and flat country, the bison is a hill animal. Their recesses and heavy sholahs are his natural home, and he never strays to any great distance from their confines.

For so bulky a beast he is a capital climber, and his neat and small hoof marks will often be discovered in precipitous spots more suitable for ibex than for any other animal. His small feet—not much larger than those of a big sambur—are a special characteristic, and will at once attract the sportsman's attention, as being apparently disproportionate to the rest of the massive frame they have to support.

At certain seasons, when the flies in the low and sheltered valleys become very troublesome, the herds often betake themselves to open tracks of grass land on the higher ranges, where the cooler temperature and stronger breezes diminish the numbers of their persecutors.

The ordinary black house fly is a terrible infliction to man and beast; he swarms everywhere, and myriads luxuriate even up to an elevation of 7000 feet. Both bison and sambur will then be found on the windward slopes of the hills.

But the enemy they dread most does not thrive at such high altitudes. He is a species of gadfly, resembling the British cleg or horse-fly, but six times as large, and is armed with a proboscis resembling an elephant's trunk on a small scale.

This scourge is the originator of "warbles," by depositing its eggs in the flesh of the bison, which subsequently turn into these maggots, and cause the victim intense pain. Sambur and elephants also suffer in this way, but the latter animal extemporises a fly whisk from a branch, which, held by his trunk, is used with deadly effect, for—like the cleg—these flies are slow in movement and soft in body, and are easily squashed. The first indication of the proximity of a herd of bison is frequently given by their strong smell, which pervades the adjacent jungle for many yards. It resembles that of milch cattle, but is far more pungent, and can be winded at a distance of over 100 yards. Unless frequently fired at, herds will generally be found in a particular locality inside a circle of about three miles diameter. This does not apply to old solitary bulls, which are nomadic as a rule, although they, too, have favourite haunts, to which they sooner or later return.

After the events recorded in the last chapter we left Poolakul on the 4th July, and marched to Toonacudavoo amid torrents of rain, which lasted all day. Here, for a fortnight, I had excellent sport in the forests all round, extending to a radius of ten miles, which was as far as we could venture from the depôt, without forming a separate camp. Bison or sambur were met with daily, the latter only being shot when meat was required. It soon became apparent that, like other kinds of big game, bison require a good deal of killing, and I lost several badly-wounded animals by the bullet striking a few inches outside the deadly spots. One day I had been tracking a very large solitary bull for several hours, but could not get a clear shot, although we had covered some ten miles of country in pursuit. As it was getting late we turned our steps homewards, and were crossing some open ground—the shikaries carrying the rifles—when a herd of bison jumped up within ten yards, and made off towards a sholah. Snatching a rifle from Atlay, I fired at the largest one visible, and he rolled over to the second barrel and lay kicking on the ground, but the two bullets from the second rifle seemed to revive him, for he got up and went off at a fair pace to a sholah, which was full of hill gooseberry and such like undergrowth, where, tracking being out of the question, we had to give him up.

A few days after this occurrence I was out in the Annagoondy direction, and hit off the rather stale trail of a herd about noon. This we followed for the best part of ten miles, and I got an easy shot at the bull just before dusk. He went down on the spot apparently dead. Thinking he was done for, I tried to stalk the herd again, as they had halted within fifty yards, being evidently unwilling to leave their leader in the lurch; but, seeing nothing but cows, I soon returned, and was amazed to see my quondam defunct friend going away very groggily with a wound close behind the off shoulder, and, as he was near side towards me when I fired, the steel tip must have gone clean through his body, probably missing the ribs. He got into some very thick stuff, where we left him lying down in an impenetrable maze of seega-kye (wait a bit thorn, a species of acacia), which he could not leave, nor could I get a glimpse of him. We were again baffled, but eventually found his remains near this spot on the 12th August, after a lapse of twenty-five days.

All the shikaries and coolies had been given extra rations of arrack and two goats to celebrate a good day's sport, but the feasting that ensued completely stopped my shooting for two days; my two servants had also joined the revellers, and had thereby neglected their work, so on the 12th July, as the Carders had not yet recovered the effects of the saturnalia, I took them for a day in the forest to smarten them up, starting about 9 a.m. for Shungum, three miles to the south, where the Government elephants were kept. Here I obtained a half-witted elephant cooly to take me to the Currian Sholah—a famous haunt for bison. On the way we struck a fresh trail, which was crossed by more tracks farther on, and we soon saw one browsing on the young shoots of a bamboo some sixty yards distant. I could not see any more of the beeves, but, from the size and dark colour, this appeared to be a bull, and, getting a nice broadside shot, I fired. Although severely wounded it galloped off, but we came upon it lying down in a dense mass of creepers about a quarter of a mile further on. It rose again, and, receiving two more shots, collapsed close by, and another bullet finished it. Much to my disappointment it turned out to be a cow, but a very fine one. As a rule one seldom gets a clear shot at bison; in the majority of cases the bullet has to penetrate many small intervening twigs which are liable to deflect it from its course, and in many parts of the forest the gloom is great, and a want of contrast between the foresight and dark hide of the animal adds to the difficulty of putting the bullet in the right spot; much of the following-up work is due to these causes. During the latter part of this performance, a small herd of three cows and a bull kept snorting and stampeding at intervals about 100 yards to our left; these we followed for two hours, but the bull never gave me a chance, so, as it was now getting on in the afternoon, and we were a long way from home, I told the cooly to show us the way back. He started up a steep hill, and, after an hour's walk, said he had lost the way, and did not know where we were. The sun was obscured by clouds, so he climbed a tree to reconnoitre, but failed to recognise any of the surrounding hills. During the day we got occasional glimpses of the sun, and I knew the bungalow lay to the north-east, and by feeling the trunks of the trees we worked in this direction till dark. There was nothing to be done but to lie down for the night. The jungle was swarming with leeches, but we found a sheet of rock and squatted there, drenched with rain (which had been falling all day) without food or liquor or even fire, as the matches were all wet, so that even a smoke was not procurable. The remorseless rain continued throughout the night; the rock was too small to allow us to stretch our legs, so we huddled together in a state of misery. In the middle of the night we heard a pack of wild dogs within a few hundred yards, and the cooly wanted to bolt to climb a tree, but I would not let him do so, explaining that as he had got us into trouble he would have to see us through it.

All shikaries declare that these jungle dogs, when in packs, are worse than wolves, and will attack anything, and I remember one morning in the Koobair district, where a pack had killed two of our buffaloes, being faced by them on approaching the carcases; but a shot or two dispersed them, which would probably not have been the case if they were not already satiated with flesh. We were lucky enough to escape the attentions of these Annamullay marauders, and at daybreak started again on our travels, and, after walking some miles, found a smouldering forest tree, which had probably been struck by lightning months before—we were thus enabled to warm ourselves, and dry our saturated clothes. For a long time we could not discover our bearings, the sun being still obscured by rain and a fog; but at last a fleeting gleam shone forth, and, directed by it, we struck a line which, after two hours' walking, took us to the edge of a glade, where the cooly declared we were again wrong, but I crossed it, and, discovering a track, followed it to Shungum, thence we followed the road to Toonacudavoo, arriving after a twenty-five hours' absence in a state of complete demoralisation, to say nothing of starvation. During the afternoon all the

Carders arrived in camp under their chief Vyapoori Moopen, and were intensely amused on hearing of our mishaps in the Currian Sholah.

Next morning we started in the same direction, and soon came on fresh signs of bison, which we followed down wind for a mile, when the herd scented us, and made off. We found their forms in the long lemon grass, still warm, indeed, I saw a cow dash off through the jungle as we approached. We pushed on through the tall sweetly-smelling lemon grass to the edge of a thick sholah, where the dim light rendered tracking very slow and difficult, eventually, having carried the trail through successfully, we emerged from the sholah, and entered an area of bamboo jungle. Atlay soon descried a fine bull, partly screened by a clump of bamboo, 120 yards distant—he was facing towards me, and, therefore, in a bad position, but, as he was evidently on the look out, I thought it better to take the chance, and fired. The bullet sounded very hard, as if it had struck wood, but I distinctly saw him stagger before rushing off. Owing to the smoke the Carders had not seen the movement, and were incredulous, becoming more so when we had followed the tracks for half a mile without finding blood. The tracks then led across the ghaut road into a very thick sholah, with an undergrowth of hill gooseberry, which, almost excluding the light, rendered it difficult to see the foresight of the rifle. We had not gone fifty yards, when Atlay pointed out the bull lying down under a large tree within fifteen yards, and evidently very sick. Kneeling down, I aimed for the heart and fired, whereupon he rose with difficulty, and rushed away with the rest of the herd, but fell again a short distance further on, where I finished him. He was a remarkably handsome bull, with good horns, and it took four men to carry his head and marrow bones to Toonacudavoo. The first shot struck within two inches of the root of the left horn, and must have had a tremendous effect on his nervous system, to cause him to collapse as he did, this circumstance also accounts for the "click" of the bullet, and absence of blood, when tracking him up. On the 21st July we started again for the Currian Sholah, both shikaries being victims of a surfeit of ibex flesh, and arrack the night previous, and consequently unable to do much work, so I took a line of country of my own choosing. About 2 p.m. we struck the fresh trail of a herd, and in half an hour sighted the bull, standing almost head on towards me, a bad position, but, thinking a steel-tipped bullet through the front of his shoulder would reach his lungs, I fired; It was a dull steamy day, without a breath of wind, and the smoke hung so much I could not see the effect of the shot, but the width of the slots showed he was the worse for wear. A mile up a steep hill took me to the edge of a glade about sixty yards broad, on the opposite side of which the herd had halted. It consisted of twelve bison, and I soon made out the bull by the wound on the shoulder, and gave him another bullet, aiming for the heart, but the uphill run had made me shaky, and it must have struck a little too high. The clearing away of the smoke revealed an awkward state of things, as the whole herd was charging me in a solid phalanx, not twenty-five yards off. I had reloaded the right barrel immediately after firing, and now gave the bull two more shots, which had not the least effect; but snatching the other rifle from Atlay—who bolted like a deer—I browned the animal that threatened me most, a huge cow, with both barrels; she turned a complete somersault, and fell, kicking, on her back within ten yards. This broke the formation, and caused immense confusion, a whirlwind of bison hurtled past—one almost knocking me down—and crashed madly away through the forest. It was a close shave, and my safety was undoubtedly due to the barricade formed by the body of the cow I had knocked over. Bison have the reputation of charging at the smoke of a shot, and they probably did so in this case, as my body would have been hidden by it at the beginning of their charge. Following up the herd, I got a shot at another bull, standing in a similar position to the first, and struck him in the shoulder, knocking him over; but he got up again and went clean away, so this shot cannot be depended upon—the amount of flesh, bone, and sinew to be traversed being enormous. The first bull did not go far, but we did not get him that night, as it became too dark to track; he was, however, found dead two days after, within a short distance of the glade where the big charge took place. The Carders would not touch the body, and as I was starting that day on a trip towards Michael's Valley, which lasted a week, taking with me all available hands, the beheading operations were deferred till my return. The carcase was then too far gone, and had to be left where it fell, for several months before the head could be removed. On the 23rd July I marched from Toonacudavoo to Perrincudavoo (Fruit Town), an old encampment of the Carders, where two very comfortable huts still existed in good preservation; we were short of meat, as the village of Annamullay had been able to yield but two fowls. Next day I shot a bison within a few miles of camp, and severely wounded another in the act of charging us, but he was conducted by two of his zenana across the River Periar, which I forgot to mention ran past our camp, and in the absence of a raft we were left lamenting on the bank. We also saw three-days-old tracks of a large herd of elephants, and many signs of spotted deer and sambur. During the day the Mulsers had constructed a bamboo raft, which was moored about a mile down the river. We crossed here next morning, and soon found tracks of a solitary tusker, which we followed for about twelve miles, but even then the droppings were several hours old, and the tracks led away from home, so we relinquished the pursuit. During this unsuccessful day we saw one large herd of bison and passed fresh tracks of several others.

A few days later we again crossed the Periar, and within a mile hit off the fresh tracks of a herd—which Atlay had walked over without noticing; these we followed to the base of a small hill covered with long grass, both the Carders being in front, when I saw what appeared to be a bull, some forty yards ahead, and slightly to the right-front, in the usual pointing attitude—nose in the air and horns almost touching the back. Directly Atlay cleared my front I fired at the forehead; he (Atlay) seemed to be much more astonished than the bison, which, wheeling round, bolted away, followed by the rest of the herd, which we had not hitherto seen. Then ensued the usual scene of finding blood on the leaves, coming on the wounded animal, &c., until Atlay took up the trail, as the other Carder was muffing it. He soon pointed out the wounded bison, about ten yards distant, lying in wait under a thick festoon of creepers, in which position I shot it, and was disappointed to find it was a cow; but the horns were very large, being more than two feet from bend to bend. We then took up the tracks of the big bull of the herd, there was no mistaking them, and we knew by their size he was an exceptionally heavy beast. After an hour we came upon the herd in a thicket of bamboos, where it was very difficult to select the bull; but after half an hour's stalking, avoiding the cows, which were very suspicious, I got two bullets into him as the herd stampeded. He was very hard hit, and we tracked him for another hour, chiefly by the blood, of which there were signs all the way; three times he started up within a few yards, but the dense jungle screened him from view, and as night was approaching we had to desist from pursuit and return to camp.

On the 2nd August two Carders brought news that this bull was lying dead near the foot of Cooramikul Mullay, a high hill, along the base of which we had been following him; they had a long story about him which I could not understand beyond the fact that he was dead. It was my last day at Perrincudavoo, and there was one beat still untried; so, as the Carders said they would get two Mulsers to bring the head to Toonacudavoo, I determined not to waste the day on the dead animal. In the evening Captain Barnett arrived, and I asked him to look out for the bull in the course of his wanderings. He did so, and found it lying at the place indicated, partly devoured by a tiger. All round the spot were signs of a desperate struggle, and there is no doubt that the tiger scenting the blood of the wounded animal had tackled him forthwith, probably when the poor beast was lying down. A tiger would hardly attack an unwounded bison. Barnett, who was a good and experienced shikari, said the bull was the largest he had ever seen, and that his horns were well over forty inches in breadth, but, owing to the effluvia, he could not measure them properly. A Carder brought me a creeper and a bamboo marked with the breadth, both of which showed it as a little over forty-two inches, but these could not be relied on.

On the 30th July I got a bison near the Poolakul Ibex Hill, after stalking it for two hours, at the end of the time getting a snap shot which went through the heart; a very large beast, with shabby horns. It rained almost incessantly from the morning of the 27th to mid-day on the 29th, resulting in our being cut off from our depôt of supply at Toonacudavoo, and, as I could not touch bison flesh on account of its strong odour, recourse was had to jungle fowl and black monkeys for the pot. The former were scarce, in fact I only got a shot at one, of which there was but little left after a 12-bore bullet had perforated him; and the latter were unpleasant things to shoot, although very good when curried. I only had nerve enough to shoot one; he was dismembered and mixed up with the fragments of the jungle-cock—and I never knew whether the food was bird or beast, it was a tasty but distinctly cannibalistic repast. One evening I strolled down to the river to examine some bison heads which had been placed in the stream to clean, and saw several good sized fish, presumably mahseer, swimming about close to them. A fishing rod and tackle having been improvised, some time was spent in unsuccessful attempts to lure them with worms. The Periar here was about forty yards broad, with a nice stream and several likely looking pools, but an alligator on the opposite bank represented some of its inmates, and dispelled the salmon river illusion it otherwise would have given rise to. My stock of hardened bullets becoming exhausted, I had to melt down the handle of an old pewter mug which had been my faithful servant on several shooting trips. From this, five bullets were cast, which subsequently accounted for three bison. Barnett had been using a Martini rifle at these animals, but was not satisfied with its performances, and no doubt the bore is too small for such heavy beasts.*

On the 3rd August I marched to Toonacudavoo, taking the Poolakul ibex hill on the way, but found no fresh tracks of ibex, nor did I fire a shot that day. My trip to Perrincudavoo had afforded capital sport, only four days having been blank ones. The weather all this time had been very wet, and, as has been already stated, we had three days on short commons; but these minor discomforts were unable to dim the pleasures of that expedition.

The undergrowth of these forests had vastly increased since my arrival, in many places the grass, creepers, cannæ, caladiums, &c., being several feet in height; the open spaces were gradually becoming choked with rank vegetation, and this not only threw great difficulties in the way of tracking by obscuring the slots of bison, but also, by increasing the amount of covert, considerably impeded the view, and the time was approaching when little could be done with any animals except wild elephants.

Laying in a fresh stock of provisions and ammunition at Toonacudavoo, I started for Poolakul on the afternoon of the 4th August, and the following morning entered the forest in a southerly direction, finding numerous four days old elephant tracks within a few hundred yards of the camp, all leading towards the cardamom jungles of Travancore, which, without the Rajah's permission, was forbidden ground. After walking some distance we found the trail of a large bull bison, and, while following it up, heard the howling of a bear not far off. A voyage of

* Although knocked down, the majority recovered and escaped. Even a 12-bore is hardly large enough for so heavy an animal.

discovery in his direction being unsuccessful, we resumed tracking the bison, but in a few minutes heard what I thought was a tiger calling to its mate. Both shikaries declared it was a tiger, and were not a bit keen on tracking it up. We could find no signs of pugs, but proceeded in the direction, and got quite close to the spot it emanated from. Suddenly a tremendous crashing took place, and the note changed. Both shikaries said "ānee," whereupon I put in elephant cartridges, loaded with $7\frac{1}{8}$ drachms of powder and hardened bullets. A few yards further on we discovered a herd of bison, which had been giving vent to these extraordinary sounds. A sufficiently clear shot not being obtainable, we followed the herd slowly, the cows, as usual, presenting the most tempting shots, and, moreover, keeping such a sharp look out, that, although we took every advantage of wind and cover, no opening occurred at the bull. The cows bellowed, snorted, and rushed away, taking the bull with them. Three of these stampedes took place in the course of a ten mile stalk, at the end of which, I got a long shoulder shot at what appeared to be the bull. Away rushed the herd again, but the wounded one lay down twice within a short distance in very thick covert, and bolted on our approach. For several miles we continued the pursuit, till we arrived on the banks of the Periar, where, instead of crossing the river, they turned up the right bank. Twice again we roused it in thick covert, but the shikaries were not to be blamed, for one could not see five yards ahead in the almost impenetrable tangle of canes and creepers. We carried on the tracks till the sun began to sink, and were proceeding down a slope covered with clumps of bamboos towards the river, when the brute suddenly charged us from our left flank. The right barrel brought it down as if shot through the brain, within

CHARGE OF THE PERIAR BISON.

twenty yards. Reloading, we proceeded to bombard it in the usual way with sticks, gradually approaching step by step. After about a minute it jumped up again, and had taken a few steps towards the river, when a bullet through the heart laid it low—a cow nearly seventeen hands high with twenty-three inch horns. The bullet, fired as it charged, struck the left horn close to its base, rolling it over as if dead, the core inside the horn being greatly damaged by the shot. Next day we started eastwards over Desperation Hill, and soon met with a herd, which was very much on the look out, and stampeded forthwith.

For two hours we followed them over hill and dale without getting a view, and then they halted on a bamboo-clad hill, and I sighted one browsing about sixty yards distant; at the same instant a large cow, starting up within thirty yards, stared fixedly in our direction; we immediately sank slowly to the ground, and remained perfectly still for some minutes, the cow still gazing at us, although she evidently had not got our wind. The further bison appeared to be the bull from its size and dark colour, but the thick covert prevented his head being seen. On firing I heard the bullet tell, and we followed up the traces for three hours, but they were too much on the alert, and never let us within one hundred yards, although the wounded one had twice laid down. At the end of that time we came to the foot of a steep hill; up which the tracks led, and, after a stiff climb for half a mile, found ourselves on a plateau, covered with thick sholah, where, within twenty yards, I saw what was evidently the bull staring out at us, head thrown back and nose projected in the usual bison fashion. It was an awkward shot, but, aiming below the level of the eyes, I pressed the trigger, but when the smoke cleared away the animal was still in the same position, and on going up we found a log of wood—part of the trunk of a tree—perforated by the bullet, in a spot which *ought* to have been adjacent to the bison's brain. Atlay had been hoaxed as well as I, and this was my only consolation during my twelve mile trek home. He told me that some years previously "cholera" (murrain) had attacked the bison, nearly exterminating them, and that he saw over one hundred carcases lying in the jungles, within a few months, of animals that had died from the disease. He said the shooting was now nearly over for the season on account of the dense undergrowth, and that he and his clan would soon be occupied with their ordinary work, collecting jungle produce, such as saffron, ginger, wild honey, and antlers shed by deer; these they sold to traders from the low country who visit these forests periodically. These Carders shift their camps when they have exhausted the products of a given portion of jungle, and sow a few wretched patches of grain in clearings near their cold weather quarters. A few days later I left the Annamullays and bade farewell to Douglas, who had been most kind in helping me in every way, and without whose co-operation nothing could have been done. Captains Clay and Borthwick, of the 79th Highlanders, arrived from Kamptee, and took my place. They had very fair sport, especially with elephants, which had been attracted from their usual haunts by the young growth of bamboos here. My subsequent operations with bison were chiefly restricted to the Muddoor and Bandipore jungles.

In June, 1881, I shot my last bison within a few miles of the travellers' bungalow at Bandipore, where I had arrived from Ootacamund. Mr. Harvey, who had come out from England on a shooting expedition, and had been here for some days, reported that the jungles were a good deal disturbed by grazing cattle, and that there were but few herds of bison in the vicinity, still he had had some sport with bears and other jānwars, including a rogue tusker, which he had fired at and wounded, and which then chased him for a considerable time, nearly catching him on several occasions, but a heavy 8-bore double-barrel eventually gave the elephant a quietus. I am writing from memory, but believe that the encounter lasted for an hour. The tusks were nice ones, but rather splintered by bullets during the heat of the engagements.

This gentleman very kindly agreed to an arrangement by which the road from Tippicado to Goondulpett was to be the march between our respective forests, his tract to lie to the west towards the Muddoor jungles, and mine eastwards towards the Billiga Rungums. Very little rain had fallen, and most of the natives were suffering from fever; moreover, there was but little growth of grass to tempt the bison from the heavy forests lying towards the Hona Matti Hills on the east, and Karkankottah to the west. With much difficulty I secured a Sholigar as shikari. He was just released from prison and was anxious for a job, and, as he knew the jungles and there was nobody else available except my hill shikari, who was quite unacquainted with these parts, I took him into my service for the trip. Starting next morning at ten o'clock we walked in a southerly direction for two hours, passing fairly fresh tracks of elephant, tiger, bison, bear, and deer, but none were recent enough to follow. None of the forest trees of the Annamullays were to be seen here, and, although it was virgin forest, the trees were stunted as a rule, looking as if the soil or climate was unsuitable to growth, but the variety of wild animals was greater than in any jungle which I had hitherto visited. This was evidenced by their tracks which were everywhere to be seen. About 1 p.m. we discovered fresh slots of four bison, and tracked them for half a mile through some bamboo scrub, whence we emerged into a large glade; at the opposite side of which in thick jungle some heavy animals were making a great crashing, the Sholigar immediately exclaiming "ānee," but they were the bison we had been tracking. A thick clump of saplings, intertwined with creepers, circular in form, and about thirty yards in diameter, was situated in the middle of the glade, and towards this we were in the act of crossing when a native, who was herding cattle some distance off in the forest beyond the bison, harangued his flock at the top of his voice, whereupon the bison, galloping towards us, entered the clump in front. The bull passed through it, appearing immediately afterwards at the edge on our side within thirty yards, snorting loudly and looking towards us, his horns festooned with the creepers, as we knelt in the middle of the open ground, where there was little if any covert. Aiming for the neck shot near the level of his right eye, I pressed the trigger, the heavy 8-bore, loaded with hardened bullet and 8 drachms of powder, knocked me over, but it did the same to the bull, who was shot through the spine, and turned his toes to the sky, never moving a yard. At the same moment the rest of the herd, consisting of two cows and a young bull, galloped past within twenty yards, but they were not worth firing at. The dead bull was a fine beast, with an indifferent pair of horns barely 30 inches in breadth. I measured him twice between uprights very carefully, and found his height to be approximately 19½ hands, viz.,

$77\frac{3}{4}$ inches; if he had been measured to the highest point of the hump, which is not vertically over the shoulder, he would have been some inches more.

A few days later all the servants and shikaries were down with fever, and I had to march to Mysore. The next news from those jungles was to the effect that Captain Chamberlayne had fired at and wounded a bison, which charged, and knocking him down, attempted to gore him on the ground. Chamberlayne, however, made good use of a strong pair of shooting boots, and gave the brute as much as he got, and, although he returned for another bout, the result was a drawn battle, both opponents, however, being considerably the worse for wear; in fact, Chamberlayne had to relinquish sporting operations for some time, and was lucky to escape with his life. In Captain Barnett's case, the bison was lying down wounded, and he fired at the shoulder, but this only seemed to put fresh vigour into the brute, which got up and charged him, knocking him over, and then gored him, but luckily only slightly, owing to the horns being very much curved; Barnett eventually shot the brute. For bison, I used a 12-bore rifle and hardened spherical bullets, propelled by six drachms of powder; but I found this was insufficient to penetrate to the lungs from the point of the shoulder—at least, it could not always be relied on to do so. I also tried a conical bullet with the same charge of powder, but on the whole the spherical one gave more satisfaction. In a broadside shot aim behind, and a shade higher, than the elbow—the hump is liable to catch the eye, and as a rule bullets are placed too high in consequence. Bison are very fond of salt licks, and it is well to make inquiries if any exist in the neighbouring jungles, and to visit them, for this will show at a glance what different kinds of game are about, as deer are just as fond of these places as bison. In these spots the earth is saturated with salt, which effloresces on the surface, and all kinds of deer travel long distances to lick the earth, and I believe to eat some of it. The paths made by game will always be found to converge towards where these licks exist. They are insignificant looking spots, the ground being merely a patch bare of vegetation for a few square yards, exposing the saline earth, which is generally a reddish clay; but there will be plenty of proof all round of how they are appreciated by deer and bison. Pig do not patronise them, probably because they do not ruminate, but the tracks of elephants will often be found at these places. Several existed in the Annamullays, and, to the best of my recollection, three were to be found between Muddoor and Tippicado. In the Nandair district of the Nizam's dominions they were also numerous, and the ambuscades of the natives, which were invariably adjacent, proved they were equally attractive to the denizens of those jungles.*

The shikaries, in jungles where elephants existed, stated that those animals, as well as bison, suffer much from intestinal worms, and that they eat great quantities of saline earth to rid themselves of these pests. Moreover, that when wounded, the elephants always travel to the nearest salt lick to plug the bullet holes with the earth, as this prevents the flies from depositing their eggs in them. The rutting season of the bison commences in the cold weather, the cows calving about the months of July and August, at which time they separate from the herds for some weeks, until their offspring are able to trot about. After some experience of herd bison, their pursuit becomes

* At every pool of water these ambuscades were also present, and those jungles are gradually becoming denuded of game.

rather monotonous, there is but little variation in the programme, and not much danger as a rule. Moreover there is great waste of meat, in the remoter jungles usually resorted to by them, owing to the absence of dhers—or other pariahs—who in jungles nearer civilisation eat up every morsel that can be found. The head as a trophy, the tail for soup, the marrow-bones and tongue, will supply the needs of most camps, and the remainder of the immense frame will only benefit the tiger or panther. The pursuit of solitary bulls is a branch of the sport which affords more excitement, and is not so much open to objection, for he is a morose and even dangerous animal, and is useless to his own species. An 8-bore double barrel rifle, burning eight drachms of powder, with a hardened bullet, would be my choice weapon for any future bison stalking. It is a more humane one than a 12-bore, fewer animals getting away to pine and die of their wounds, and, if elephants were encountered, it ought to acquit itself well enough, in the absence of a 4-bore.

MY LAST BISON.

CHAPTER XI.

THE ELEPHANT (*Elephas Indicus*).

Distribution of—Shooting prohibited in 1871—Damage caused by—Reward formerly offered for—Elephant pits—Rogue elephants—Dangers of elephant shooting—Where to aim—Large bores desirable—Steel tipped bullets—Major Gordon Cumming—System inaugurated by—Advantage of learning jungle dialects—Start with Cumming to shoot elephants—Scene of operations—Commencement of encounter—One tusker killed — A stern chase—A record shot — Narrow shave—Death of second tusker—Tusks disfigured—Beat for sambur—Routed by cow elephant—Return to Bangalore—Baffled Sybarites—How to scare a herd—Woodcraft—Difference between habits of elephants and bison.

THE haunts of the wild elephant in Southern India comprise the virgin forests of Coorg, Canara, the Wynaad, Coimbatore, Mysore, and Travancore, and their hill ranges, together with the fringes of lesser jungle which abut on the cultivated lowlands in those districts. They are, in fact, identical with those inhabited by the bison. In the forests near the Godavery the wild elephant is also found, and when tiger shooting in those districts, news was occasionally brought to camp of their presence in the vicinity.

Since the ukase issued by the Madras Government in 1871 against the killing of wild elephants, and the subsequent cessation of kheddah operations, these animals have increased enormously in the forests of Southern India, and the outcry of the ryots cultivating lands adjoining these tracts has become louder in proportion to the enhanced damage sustained by their crops each successive year. A small herd of a dozen elephants will destroy many acres of rice or jowari * fields during a nocturnal raid lasting but a few hours, not only by eating it, but by tramping it down, for, although when in the jungle they are much addicted to travelling in single file, directly they debouch into arable land they extend on a broad front, a formation better suited for foraging, as otherwise the leaders of the herd would annex all the tit-bits. These visits will almost to a certainty be repeated by succeeding herds, which have a habit of following the same routes as their predecessors, and which are adhered to from year to year. A few years previous to the veto against the shooting of elephants, a Government reward of seventy rupees was actually paid for every elephant killed, and great numbers were destroyed by native shikaries with huge guns, fired from a tripod by slow match. As one elephant per annum was sufficient to keep the man living in comparative luxury for the whole of that time, some of the jungle wallahs made a good thing of it, especially as they also used pitfalls, which were dug in the routes by which the elephants proceeded during the rains on their annual visit to the bamboo jungles, in search of the young shoots, of which they are very fond. These still exist in some jungles, and are twelve feet long, eight broad, and fifteen feet deep. A stick is placed across the pit to break the fall of the elephant when it is intended to catch him alive, but the depth is so great that the unfortunate animals generally succumb to internal injuries or broken limbs. I have a dim recollection of seeing some pits in the Annamullays, in which a pointed stake had been driven to kill the animal, which, if a tusker, occasionally escaped by digging down the sides of the pits, and

* Same as cholum—a species of millet.

gradually filling them with the earth thus displaced. The pits were arranged in groups of four or five, two usually being in front, and one on each flank to intercept those that bolted on the collapse of the leading elephant. Bison and sambur were not unfrequently victimised by these contrivances. The Mysore Government also prohibited the killing of elephants in the same year (1871), and since then have only sanctioned enterprises against "rogues," which are solitary male elephants addicted to infesting the vicinity of roads, where they interrupt the traffic and frequently kill any human being they may meet. A few of these brutes were on the warpath almost every year in the Mysore jungles. One was a well-known muckna (tuskless male), and lorded it over the natives in the Karkancottah jungles. Several men had been killed by him. It was stated that he had been wounded by a sahib, and that this had the effect of making him an implacable enemy to all mankind. Mucknas are credited with being far more dangerous than the ordinary tusker, and it was one of these brutes that killed Wedderburn in the old muzzle-loading days, in the Wynaad jungle near Tippicado.

In 1880 and 1881 a rogue elephant was hanging about the main road from Mysore to Ootacamund, near this place (Tippicado); his beat extended as far as Bandipore to the north, and to Madoor * on the west. I obtained a "licence to shoot rogue elephants" through the kind offices of Colonel Pearse (who was himself a thorough sportsman), my intention being to first tackle the Tippicado rogue—on account of his tusks—and then to try conclusions with the Karkancottah muckna. Owing to the exigencies of the service, leave could only be obtained for short spells at a time, and on arrival at Bandipore he

* Or "Muddoor."

was invariably reported to be either at Muddoor or Tippicado; next day, on reaching Muddoor, he would be on the return journey to either of the other places, and in the journeys to and fro we never met. Then I got a bullock-cart, and patrolled the road from Bandipore to Tippicado, backwards and forwards for two days, in the hope of "drawing" him, but it was useless; finally I tried strategy, by camping at Gopaulswamy, a position which enabled me to act on Interior Lines, but an interview could never be arranged. Moreover, these manœuvres occupied so much of my leave that the Karkancottah rogue could not be visited on either occasion. The ordinary wild elephants seemed to know that they were protected, and were very much *en evidence*, in short obtrusively familiar, being quite a nuisance when stalking bison. But, although they were forbidden game, it was most interesting to study their habits when bison were not forthcoming. The few sportsmen who have had experience in this branch of shikar (they can be counted easily on the fingers of one hand), with one notable exception, are of opinion that it is the most risky type of sport, and all have had several narrow escapes with wounded elephants. The exception referred to was the late General Douglas Hamilton, who declared bison shooting was more dangerous, and to this opinion—founded on great experience—much deference is due. As a rule, the Indian sportsman aims to strike the brain, which is small and oval in section—one foot long, and nine inches in breadth. It lies far back, and low in the head, and, on account of its position, the bullet, before reaching it, must penetrate a considerable thickness of bone and tissue; therefore the projectile should be hardened, and propelled by a large charge of powder. The front shot is the favourite one;

the mark is well defined, and the path to the brain offers but little impediment to penetration. Aim is taken below the centre of the bump just over the trunk, when the elephant is facing the firer, on level ground, the drawback to the shot being that it is seldom offered. If the elephant is on higher ground, aim must be taken lower, and *vice versâ*, the nearer the sportsman is to the animal the greater must be the allowance for difference of level. The temple shot—half way between eye and ear—aim so as to break in half an imaginary stick joining the centres of the ears—an angle of forty-five degrees with the plane of the length will ensure this. The ear-shot—aim at right angles through the ear-hole, not always an easy mark in the gloom of the forest. The rear shot is in prolongation of the temple shot; try to break the stick in half by firing from rear to front, at an angle of forty-five degrees with the plane of the elephant's length.

The rules regarding differences of level apply to all these shots. The eyes of the elephant are fair guides to the level of his brain, except when the firer is on higher ground. On level ground the eyes are below the brain, but the tendency is to aim too high, and the heavy charges used, increase the error. The elephant's sight is bad, but his sense of smell is very keen, be careful therefore to keep to leeward of him; try the wind frequently with tobacco ashes, bits of dry grass, &c., and you will have no difficulty in getting within twenty yards of him, in ordinary ground; do not fire at a greater range, but if you can get within ten yards do so, but don't go nearer.

These rules have been framed on the experiences of several sportsmen who have had practical proof of their truth; one of them (Captain Buckle, R.A.) spoke of a fifth shot which once saved his life, when an infuriated tusker was almost on the top of him, viz., through the roof of the mouth. When an elephant charges with trunk curled and head raised, as is sometimes their custom, few rifles can shoot hard enough to reach the brain, as in addition to the bony portion of the skull by which it is protected, the trunk must first be perforated by the projectile, but in most cases he would be staggered by the impact, and give an opening for the left barrel; if, however, the firer was on higher ground this difficulty would not exist, as he would then be above the level of the trunk. Elephants are sometimes killed by the shot behind the shoulder, but a large bore and heavy charge of powder are of course advisable, if not absolutely necessary, for this. I once tried it with a 12-bore rifle, burning $7\frac{1}{8}$ drachms of powder, behind a steel-tipped conical bullet, and, greatly to my surprise, found that the bullet and tip had parted company, the latter emerging behind the shoulder on the opposite side. The late Frank Gordon Cumming, who was with me at the time, and had put two bullets into the same tusker's head (which was hidden from me), considered that the projectile had passed between the ribs, this being the only way to account for the extraordinary penetration—fuller particulars of this incident are given further on in this chapter. On several subsequent occasions the same thing occurred with bison, when the charge of powder was but six drachms. The steel tip was smaller in diameter than the rest of the projectile, and was very sharp at the point, but its base had not much hold on the lead (vide illustration *a* on next page, in which the shaded portion represents the tip), some that were cut out of bison had assumed the shape *b*, when propelled by $2\frac{1}{2}$ drachms of powder from my second rifle. These had only penetrated a few inches, and were worse than useless, merely goading the unfortunate animal. It is possible that the heavier charges of powder caused the bullet to mushroom sufficiently to liberate the sharp and hard tip, which would fly forward with the same velocity as the bullet at the moment of liberation, its shape and smaller

(*a*)

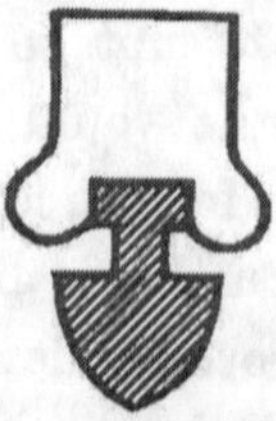

(*b*)

surface enabling it to penetrate further than the rest of the projectile, which was of ordinary soft lead, for when casting them it was assumed that, as the tip would bear the brunt of penetration, hardened lead behind would be superfluous.

I was first introduced to wild elephants when quartered at Bangalore in 1870 by Gordon Cumming, who then held an important position in the Mysore Commission. He had perfected an Intelligence Department for shikar purposes, by means of which immediate news of the presence of all big game within fifty miles of that station was at once transmitted to him. He had previously held a similar appointment at Shimoga, where—by inaugurating a like method of obtaining "khubber"—he had developed the sporting capabilities of that district to the utmost extent, and had had capital sport. He was a fair shot with a rifle, moderately so with a gun, and plucky—and as cool as a cucumber—when engaged with big game. Of course with his exceptional advantages, he had acquired a good knowledge of the jungle and the habits of its inmates. At that time I had already made my *début* with tigers, panthers, bears, &c., but knew nothing about bison or elephants. Shooting was my craze; every day of my leave was devoted to either gun or rifle, and when off duty in Cantonments, all spare time was given to rifle practice or small game shooting, the study of anatomy so far as it related to the structure of elephants' heads, and the vital points of wild animals generally, likewise to a colloquial knowledge of Hindostani, Tamil, Telugoo, and Burmese, with a view to shikar expeditions, an acquaintance with these dialects being of incalculable advantage to the sportsman when in remote districts, where, to be successful, he must be his own interpreter. Before proceeding to any jungle district, even a few weeks' study of its dialect is the best preliminary to ensure good sport. Several of my friends were also devoted to the jungle—how we used to long for the leave season to come round!—although, without exception, we were zealous soldiers and fond of our profession.

After muster parade on the 30th June, 1870, I started on ten days' leave of absence with Gordon Cumming, to look for some elephants which were reported to have arrived near Hooliya, a small jungle hamlet some fifty miles south of Bangalore. A drive of thirty-six miles took us to the travellers' bungalow at Kankanhulli, where we found that all our provisions and liquor had been sent on to Hooliya by the amildar,* but it was too late in the day to continue the journey, most of which led through a rocky country covered with scrub jungle; so we slept there, and, starting early next morning, arrived in our camp in Hooliya about noon, after a fatiguing march of fourteen miles, most of which was performed on foot, the ground being too rough and jungly to use our horses. The head shikari met us on our arrival, reporting that the elephants—two

* District native official.

tuskers and a cow—were about two koss distant, in some thick jungle towards the River Cauvery, and that he had left two jungle wallahs to watch them. We thereupon held a council of war, deciding to tiffin and start after them without loss of time, as they could not be depended on to stay another night in their present quarters, and might be forty miles away if we waited until next morning.

A walk of over an hour through park-like undulating country, took us to a lonely valley surrounded by steep hills, and about one mile in breadth, through the middle of which a prettily-wooded stream wound down to the Cauvery. The scouts, immediately descending from their trees, came forward to report that the elephants, after drinking, bathing, and skylarking in a small pond, had betaken themselves to feed in a dense thicket of the smaller kind of bamboo, which fringed the stream about half a mile below us. Descending into the valley, we first visited the pond, which was not more than twenty yards square. The margin had once been covered with barroo reeds, but these the elephants had demolished ; the place was poached up in every direction by their tracks, the steep banks had also been scaled, and high jinks had evidently been going on all round; indeed, the jungle wallahs reported that this was a honeymooning trip, and that the pond had been the scene of both love and war. Also that the tuskers were rival suitors, and had had frequent indecisive battles, as, although differing in size, the smaller bull had larger tusks than his opponent, which subsequently proved to be true. We then took the tracks up to the thicket, and soon heard the cracking of the bamboos as they were munched by the elephants. Creeping forward we got to within twenty yards of them, but the covert was too dense to see anything, so, having ascer-

"THE ELEPHANTS, NOW IN FULL VIEW, HALTED WITHIN TWENTY YARDS."

tained that there was little or no wind, we lay down at the edge of a small glade, towards which the trio were feeding, with our second rifles on the ground beside us. The crunching of the bamboos got louder and louder by degrees, and at last a huge brown mass, with a pair of gleaming tusks emerged from the jungle on the opposite side of the glade—some thirty yards across, and smelling danger sounded the alarm by striking the end of his trunk against the ground, thus emitting a metallic noise resembling a log of timber falling on hard ground.* His companions then drew up beside him, the female in the centre. After a minute's deliberation they slowly advanced, but in a hesitating manner, trying the wind with their trunks and evidently suspicious of danger. Each man was to take the tusker next him, the cow was not to be fired at, we had a final look at our cartridges, full cocked the rifles, and opened the cartridge pouches so as to be ready for reloading. The elephants now in full view had halted within twenty yards. A rifle in each hand we both jumped to our feet, and ran forward to engage them. At a close range I fired three shots at my tusker's head and one for the other tusker's heart as he swerved off to my right front, his head being obscured by the cow's stern. They all crashed off through the bamboos, closely pursued by us. Seventy yards further on, Cumming's tusker collapsed stone dead in a kneeling position. In addition to his shots in the head, the steel tip of my bullet had, as already mentioned, passed through the body in the line of the heart. After a minute we continued the chase—a stern chase and destined to be a long one—and soon afterwards saw the shadowy outlines of the two

* This noise can be heard at a distance of two hundred yards.

elephants who had halted to wait for their companion. As we advanced they moved into an adjacent glade where we again opened fire but without effect, for charging off they crossed the stream into another thicket of "Seega kye"* and bamboos, through which we valorously followed till our clothes were torn to rags. This burst lasted for ten minutes, when we emerged into more open forest for some hundreds of yards, until we again found ourselves in a hopeless brake of male bamboo, so thick that it was impossible to see five yards in front. The tracks separated here, so we did the same, each of us following his own line, it was a regular maze, but by following in the elephant's wake, a view was obtainable for about ten yards in front.

When fifty yards inside the thicket, a loud crashing close to my right was followed by the apparition of the tusker, charging along the back track. He was twelve yards from me, but the right barrel missed him clean, the bullet cutting a bamboo stem just over his head (a record shot). The left barrel, fired when he was almost on the top of me, luckily turned him a little, and he passed within a few feet on my left, and thundered away through the bamboos like an express train. Done to a turn I crawled out of the thicket and threw myself upon the ground, where Cumming, having heard my shots, soon arrived, dead beat also. The stream was close at hand where a drink and wet handkerchiefs round our heads soon revived us. We had a good laugh over my curious shot, and a useful rest of ten minutes before continuing the fray. To avoid the bamboos we then made a detour and soon struck the trail of both the elephants, which led us along the right bank of the stream for two hundred

* Thorny acacia.

yards where it crossed and entered another dense patch of jungle. On the opposite side of this, we viewed both animals heading towards our left, and, running forward, poured in a volley, a shot from Cumming's 8-bore muzzle-loader bringing the tusker to his knees, but he got up again and bolted away as fresh as paint. Cumming had to halt to reload, but I pushed on and was slowly gaining on the tusker, whose ponderous hind-quarters were about thirty yards ahead. The jungle now was easy going, a few scattered clumps of bamboo and no undergrowth, but the position of the tusker disclosed no vulnerable point.

At length, losing patience, the right barrel was fired at the leviathan target in front, in order to provoke a charge; the effect was magical; round he came screaming with rage, ears cocked, and trunk uplifted. He was on slightly higher ground, and came down the slope like a runaway locomotive, but his trunk was still in the way. When about twenty yards distant an overhanging bamboo caused him to lower it, and to expose the bump. As the trigger was pressed, I heard Cumming's bullet—fired from thirty yards behind me—whistle past and "thud" on the tusker, who, swerving slightly to my left, crashed into a bamboo, and fell dead within twenty yards, getting another shot from the 8-bore as he collapsed. The scouts had spoken the truth, for this tusker was rather smaller than the first, but had longer and more massive tusks; they were cut out very badly by the coolies, who, although specially warned, left some nine inches of each in the skull. Cutting them out is always a dangerous operation; it is much better to leave them for some days until decomposition sets in, when they can be drawn out without difficulty. So far as we could ascertain, by measuring the portions cut out, each tusk of the lighter pair was 42 inches in length, and the others about 48 inches each; and some months afterwards, when the embedded portions were brought into Bangalore, we found that our estimate was approximately correct. When they are not cut out on the spot a piquet of three watchers should be detailed to camp in the vicinity until the tusks can be extracted, otherwise they will probably be stolen, even in the remotest jungles.

Next day, when beating for sambur, the coolies encountered the cow elephant, which was in a shocking temper, and charged them vigorously. The beat had to be stopped, and, although much inclined for another scrimmage, and a good deal annoyed by the interruption, we decided to leave her unmolested. Poor lady! she had lost both her lovers. The tuskers' feet having been brought into camp, the tissue and gristle—which was very much like caoutchouc—were with difficulty scooped out, after many hours' labour; they were then coated internally with arsenical soap, filled with charcoal, and taken to Cantonments, where they were transformed into foot-stools and cigar-boxes. The tails mysteriously disappeared, having been removed and secreted by some of our followers, who believe the hairs to be a potent talisman in certain love philtres. One of the skulls was brought to me in Cantonments several months afterwards, when the flesh, &c., had disappeared, eventually finding its way to Europe with a friend, whose regiment relieved us at Bangalore. We had heard that the baked foot of an elephant was a dish for a Lucullus, and reasoned that the tongue would be at least as toothsome, if not more so. Both tongues were accordingly put into pickle, and taken to Bangalore, where, together with some bears' hams, which we had shot at Sawandroog, about thirty miles distant from Cantonments, they formed the nucleus of a shikar luncheon at our mess some months afterwards; the tongues, however, proved to be impervious to any knife in the establishment, being tougher than indiarubber; the bears' hams, too, although carefully injected with brine, had become tainted near the bone, so the baffled Sybarites had to be satisfied with more civilised food.

Cholera broke out in the camp at Hooliya, the day following the sambur drive; we therefore returned to Kankanhully, where, getting "khubber" of a tiger and bears we had an unsuccessful beat on the 4th of July,* returning to Bangalore the following day. The news of our success had preceded us, but some jealous friend started a rumour that we had shot Commissariat elephants, and we got unmercifully chaffed about it for a long time afterwards, many people believing the report to be true. If it is desired to move a herd of elephants that you may not fire at, but which are in the way, when bison stalking for instance, give them your wind, from some distance not less than 100 yards; if you approach nearer, be prepared to receive the charge of a cow, for they are always more pugnacious than the bulls, being solicitous for the safety of their calves. Several of my friends have been thus charged, and obliged to shoot the cow in self-defence.

When on the march the tuskers are usually in rear of a herd; at other times on the flanks, but seldom with the main body, as the cows and younger taskers seem to bore them.

When to windward of a herd you wish to scare, test the strength of the wind, and estimate how long the

* In a vast expanse of scrub jungle and boulders which stretched away to the Denkanicotta forests.

taint will take to reach them; the current of air is sometimes so faint that it barely travels at the rate of two miles in the hour. Experiments of this kind are always interesting, and knowledge thus acquired may prove useful.

One afternoon in the Annamullays, I got a bull bison by the exercise of woodcraft of this nature. The herd was feeding in a valley, down which there was an almost imperceptible drift of wind, as is often the case in such situations, we estimated it to be moving at the rate of about fifty yards per minute; the bison were in an open space devoid of covert, but on the windward side a narrow belt of bamboos, about fifty yards long, ran out from the surrounding forest to within easy distance of the bull. To reach that point, however, it was necessary to pass to windward, and within forty yards of, three cows, on the hither side of this promontory, therefore, nearly a minute was available to stalk and fire at the bull after passing them. The calculation was correct, but it was touch and go, for, just before pressing the trigger, the nearest cow got the wind from the spot I had passed a minute before, too late, however, to save the life of her lord and master.

Elephants and bison are often found in the same tracts of jungle, the natural food of both being the bamboo; but the former animal is more nomadic in his tendencies, and does not adhere to a particular locality for any length of time, as is customary with the latter. One reason for this is, that a herd of elephants will exhaust and destroy the forage in a given district more quickly than ten times as many bison. The elephant also differs from the bison in his predilection for raiding grain crops in cultivated land, which the latter animal never ventures to do, owing to his intense aversion to the presence of man and his surroundings. The elephant, on the contrary, is not so prejudiced, especially when he is a solitary one, when he often continues to graze in spite of all the efforts of the watchers to scare him.

CHAPTER XII.

THE ELEPHANT (*Elephas Indicus*).

Expedition to Thandi—Scarcity of water—Cicely—Expedition to Perrabyoo—Our hut wrecked by elephants—We get a facer—Flight of the herd—Carders fear of elephants—Aversion to tracking—Staunch with tiger—Track up tiger—The Javalee tuskers—Two exciting adventures—Elephant tracking—Solitary males—Their habits—Strike trail of—Atlay's mendacity—Skirmish with a sow—Gun carrier bolts—Advance to attack—Atlay bolts—The encounter—Get front shot—Tusker decamps—Is found dead—Tribal feud—Murrain—Pitfalls—Kheddah elephants—Clothes for elephant shooting—The foot shot—Lines of retreat to be selected—To harden bullets—Excitement of elephant shooting—The Hassanore tusker—Primary attack fails—Is followed up and shot.

THE Ceylon and Burmese elephants are stated to be identical with the Indian animal, but, for some unexplained cause, those of Ceylon are tuskless—or nearly so—only one elephant out of three hundred being a "dant wallah." * This peculiarity does not, however, extend to the elephant of Burmah, the percentage of tuskers there being the same as in India.

When in Burmah in 1876 I had two trips after elephants. The first was a solitary expedition to a village named Thandi, on a delta of the Irrawaddy, south-east of Rangoon, where a herd were in the habit of drinking at a brackish pool, in the middle of a vast savannah of kine

* Tusker.

grass, which was surrounded by a belt of impervious jungles, some ten miles distant. As Thandi was several miles from this drinking place, I decided to camp nearer to it, under a solitary bābool bush, on which a rug was hung to act as a tent. The elephants came to drink the second night, but got a slant of our wind, and made off to the jungles, without being fired at. They did not return the next night, and, as the supply of drinking water had been exhausted that day, we started early next morning on our return journey, in a Burmese boat, nearly mad with thirst, which was not assuaged until we reached Thandi about midday. I had some good cicely* shooting on the river, which was the only redeeming feature of that trip.

The next expedition was by the Pegu river to Kayengan, where we (a party of four) arrived, after a fourteen hours' journey on a steam launch. Early next morning a message was received by the Deputy Commissioner—one of our party—to the effect that a hut which had been constructed for us, was attacked and wrecked by the elephants. They were furthermore reported to be very vicious, charging everybody who approached them.

This good news pulled us through a long day's march, until, on nearing Perrabyoo about 6 p.m., we visited a pool where the elephants were accustomed to drink, and found the dead body of a cow elephant, which had been shot that afternoon by a Burman. She was one of the herd we were in search of. This was a facer to all who were acquainted with the habits of wild elephants, but some of us lay down to rest full of hope for the morrow. Next morning, however, the elephants had departed clean out

* Dendrocygna (whistling teal).

of the district, being scared by the death of their comrade. So the rest of our leave was devoted to themyng, daray, and small game of sorts. The Burman's bullet was beautifully placed. The shot had been a frontal one, and the lower edge of the lump had been perforated in the centre, exactly the right spot for a man of low stature and firing on level ground to hit. All the jungle tribes who live in elephant country are much more afraid of those animals than of tigers or bison. The Carders, in particular, were very lukewarm about tracking them up, and pointing out the burrowings of a beetle, which deposits its eggs under the warm droppings, would declare it was useless to follow the trail, as the elephants were miles ahead, and were travelling at speed, &c., &c. Knowing something about tracking, I was inexorable on these occasions. As we approached the herd their apprehension increased, the climax being reached on sighting the game, when they became useless, and could not be trusted to carry a rifle. One of them (Atlay Moopen) had been in the service of General Michael, a famous elephant shot, and therefore he probably had no faith in such small deer as me, but he was staunch at bison, and he once tracked a tiger up to the carcase of a bison which had been shot a few days previously, and then carried the pugs on to a thick clump of bushes, fifty yards distant, where we expected to find the brute. The tiger was there, but when he appeared, Atlay stood his ground like a man, not flinching in the least; indeed, he ran forward with me to try to intercept the brute before he reached some thick stuff further off, but we failed to do so, and as we only got a glimpse of him now and then as he crept quickly through the grass, he got clear off without being fired at. A few days before my departure from Toonacudavoo Captains Clay and

Borthwick, of the 79th Highlanders, had arrived on leave of absence from Kamptee, and on my departure took Atlay over as head tracker. I warned them that he was reliable on all occasions except when tuskers were concerned, and sometime afterwards received an account of their sport, and of Atlay's behaviour, with which they were much disgusted, as whenever elephants were encountered he executed a strategic movement to the rear, ā most provoking occurrence when one's spare rifle also vanishes with the truant. They had good sport with elephants, but the grass was too long for successful bison stalking. Moreover, these animals had been much worried, and were extremely wary, as Major Barnett and I had been having excellent sport there for some time previous. A friend told me of a narrow shave he once had with a tusker in the Jāvalee Hills. Two very old tuskers had been there for years, and various sportsmen had tried to annex them from time to time, but all declared that their skulls had become impervious to bullets, owing to ossification of the cellular parts of the skull close to the brain, which sets in as these animals increase in age. The natives told him that, although repeatedly fired at, the elephants invariably returned to their favourite haunts after some lapse of time. He accordingly went down and fired at and wounded one of the tuskers, but the pair went away as usual, seemingly not much the worse for wear. Some months afterwards he repeated his visit, and again wounded one of the tuskers, which pursued him until he was almost dead beat, when he fell, or threw himself into a hollow in the ground, the elephant passing on, luckily without seeing him. He thus owed his life to the defective vision of the animal.

This was pretty close work, but another friend of mine had a far more thrilling experience. He was quartered at the time at Bangalore with the 16th Lancers, and during an expedition to the jungles of Southern Mysore, he had fired at and wounded a tusker, which, although severely hit, charged, and chased him through some bamboo jungle. Unfortunately the elephant had his wind, and, although several times blinked by clumps of bamboos, the animal invariably found him out again, and finally was on the point of catching him, when he managed to double round a big bamboo, but his further flight was barred by a rock, alongside which the tree was growing. He now jammed himself into a corner, but the tusker scented him out, and made several thrusts at him with his tusks, most providentially missing him every time. The animal then retired, probably imagining he had killed his antagonist, or he may have been blinded or stupefied by the shot. The latter seems a likely solution, as under ordinary circumstances his trunk would have been used to drag the victim out, in order to trample him to death.

Provided the trail of a herd is struck about midday, and is not more than six hours old, it ought to be followed up, even if leading straight away from camp, for elephants generally rest for several hours when the sun is high, and do not recommence feeding until three o'clock in the afternoon. For instance, if at noon a six hours' old trail is hit off, the elephant would have had four hours' feeding (on the march) before the daily halt, about 10 a.m., and in that time would have covered about six miles, therefore three hours are available to catch the herd up before they move again from the halting place, some six miles distant. Another way of looking at the problem is that, in addition to the morning's stroll of, say twelve miles, another six miles, plus the distance from the finish to camp, must be added for this enterprise, exclusive of that covered after touch has been obtained of the tusker; but this is a feature of the sport, and some keen shikaries will often camp on the trail, continuing the pursuit next day. Solitary males in cool weather frequently dispense with the midday "snooze," and continue to travel throughout the day, feeding as they go along. My last encounter in the Annamullays was with a wanderer of this sort, not far from Poolakul. At that time (August, 1871), the law forbidding the shooting of elephants was actually in force, but I had been in the heart of the jungles for the best part of the preceding six months, and knew nothing about it.

The elephants were just beginning to emerge from the unexplored recesses of the mountains, their refuge during the hot weather, to make their annual foray in search of the young herbage, bamboo sprouts, &c., in the forest south of Toonacudavoo, the general line of march being by Poolakul, towards the cardamom jungles in the Travancore country, which was forbidden ground. It was therefore necessary to intercept them before they crossed the boundary of British territory, a river some ten miles west of Poolakul. Starting early one morning in a southerly direction, we walked for several hours without finding any fresh tracks of bison, but about noon struck the trail of a large solitary elephant, apparently over six hours old. The tracks of the fore feet measured four feet eight inches clear round the circumference, and as twice this is equal to the height, he was nine feet four inches at least. The shikaries, as usual, were not keen for the undertaking, pointing out that the tracks were stale, and that they were taking us away from camp towards the Travancore march, which was then some eight miles distant; but I insisted on following him for a few hours, believing he would rest for some time in the middle of the day. At the end of an hour we reached the brink of a stream running through a tract of bamboos, the foot prints led down to a salt lick in the steep bank overhanging the water; this had delayed him for a considerable time, he had wandered about and returned to it again, and the red earth bore tracks which proved he was no muckna, but a fine tusker, as my hand could fit easily into the grooves made by his tusks in the soft clay. Thence for another hour we pushed along quickly through the bamboos, finding at intervals remains of sprouts which had been devoured by him, some portions being over six feet long, and as thick as a man's leg. This was a good omen, as it signified delay, although on the other hand the fragments were covered with small insects, and the beetles had raised great mounds of earth close by the droppings. Into the latter Atlay would thrust his foot, and after remaining pensive for some seconds would murmur "ratri" (last night) in a despairing way, which made me long for Pochello, or Kistiah, or Baloo, or any of the plucky and sanguine Deccan shikaries, instead of this listless aborigine. On leaving the bamboos we entered an open part of the forest, with thick patches of cannæ dotted about, and encountered a sow with a litter, which not only barred the way, but twice charged up to within twenty yards without any provocation, for we had halted directly we saw her. However, she retired after the second demonstration, stopping at intervals and trotting back to see that we had not moved.

These beasts are a horrid nuisance when stalking, but it is better to be bullied by them than to alarm the jungle by firing. An hour later, we were stepping over the trunk of a large tree, which had been partly burnt, and I was pointing out to Atlay that some ashes which had been brushed off the elephant's feet, as he passed over, were quite fresh, and had not been washed away by a recent shower, when the second Carder—who was a few yards in advance — came rushing back the picture of terror, and exclaimed "Āni"—then pushed the rifle he had been carrying into Atlay's hand, and bolted to the rear. We advanced twenty yards, to the edge of a glade, at the opposite side of which, calmly munching a bamboo, stood the tusker eighty yards off. The glade was full of elephant creeper* and longish grass. I then inquired how the wind was. Atlay caught up some heavy leaves, and let them fall; this convinced me that he was suffering from his companion's complaint, and he ought to have been forthwith deprived of his rifle and sent to the rear. There was hardly a breath of air, and I proposed stalking him for the front shot, but Atlay recommended the ear—so I crept cautiously forward, and got behind a large tree within a dozen yards of the tusker, who showed over two feet of ivory, indicating that his tusks were about five feet long. He fed slowly past towards the left, but did not give an opening for the temple shot, his stern being towards me, and I had no confidence in the rear-to-front shot, at the back of the ear—although as he halted to eat another young bamboo shoot—this was offered most temptingly. At this stage I glanced round to see that my second rifle was at hand, but to my intense disgust found that the perfidious Atlay had withdrawn from the competition, and had taken it off with him! Five minutes elapsed without a satisfactory chance for a shot—except one, when he suddenly turned round and examined me intently, for about twenty seconds, during which

* Bauhinia.

trying interval, averting my eyes, I remained perfectly steady; this was from force of habit, for, as a rule, it is the best course to adopt, but in this case it was folly, seeing that the front shot was overlooked, and that in all probability aim could have been taken and the shot fired before he moved. Being satisfied with his inspection he recommenced feeding, and shortly after turned broadside on, exposing the ear shot; in the gloom of the forest the ear-hole was indistinct, but I could wait no longer, so aimed steadily, and fired. He first went a header into the bamboos, and remained motionless for some seconds, leaning against their thick stems; then, recovering himself, he rushed over an adjacent small tree, subsiding against a larger one, which cracked with his enormous weight, as he leaned his body against it, his legs inclined outwards, at an angle to the ground. Although not more than twenty yards distant, he was facing away, so to fire would have been useless. This was a good opportunity to reload; the paper cartridges, however, had become so swollen from damp that they would not enter the breech,* which was rather awkward; he soon revived, and, cocking his ears, began to try the wind with his trunk, and evidently sniffed the "tainted gale," for he advanced, encountering a tree on the way, through the side of which he pushed one of his tusks. I now stepped into the open, to get a clearer shot; on he came, in a shuffling sort of way, without elevating his trunk, but clearly intent on business; and when within ten yards I fired for the bump, and down he went on his knees—weak though the second rifle was, it would have been welcome then. The tusker soon recovered his legs, and, turning about, retired very groggily, cannoning against the trees that came in his

* Brass cases were not made in those days.

CHARGE OF THE POOLAKUL TUSKER.

way; he was not blinded by the shot, but simply dazed, though he had sense enough left to cross the Travancore river close by—up the opposite bank of which his track led into the territory of the Rajah, where we could not encroach. Atlay reappeared simultaneously with the elephant's retreat, declaring that if a herd had been there—instead of a solitary rogue—he would have stuck to me all the time. The scene of the skirmish was revisited on the way back; the blood that had fallen from the first wound was in gouts resembling liver, the range being nine yards; the second shot was fired at less than twelve yards range, but to this day I cannot tell where either bullet struck, although it is certain they were both very close to the brain. Four days later two Carders came in to report that a Mulser they had met the day before, had brought information of a dead tusker, which had been found towards Nilliambaddy by some jungle-wallahs, who had cut out and kept the tusks. Atlay was sent for, and declared that it was within two miles of where our scrimmage occurred, adding that his clan were not on good terms with the natives of those parts. I was incredulous, but promised that if the tusks were brought in a good reward would be given. Two Carders and the Mulser started off that day to negotiate for them, but after an absence of two days returned empty-handed, and apparently rather the worse for wear, stating that a bargain could not be struck, and that the possessors of the tusks had given them a sound thrashing; this led to a feud, which culminated in a free fight some months later, in which two men lost their lives.

If an elephant is badly wounded, and goes away, as this tusker did, he very seldom succumbs to his wounds; but occasional cases have occurred of their doing so, probably from loss of blood. How this could result from a head shot, it is difficult to say; perhaps an artery may have been cut, the hæmorrhage from which might not prove immediately fatal in the case of so huge an animal. Some years ago an account of an elephant's death from the bite of a cobra appeared in an Indian newspaper, and, to the best of my recollection, nearly twenty-four hours elapsed before the animal died; whereas, in the case of a human being, death supervenes in about the same number of minutes. Atlay, the Carder shikari, informed me that in the year 1867, in the Annamullays, when great numbers of bison died from murrain, many elephants also suffered from the same disease, and that he got three hundred rupees for a pair of tusks he then took from a dead bull elephant. In those days they were in the habit of catching elephants in pitfalls, the remains of which still existed in many parts of these forests, as well as in the Tippicado district of the Wynaad.

The Kheddah operations by Sanderson supplied great numbers of elephants to the Government, and put a stop to the system of pitfalls; but when in Bangalore in 1881, I was informed that the last animal of his first catch of elephants (numbering over fifty), had died that year; and, as they had not survived ten years' captivity, there would appear to be something wrong in this method of capture. I am unable to vouch personally for these facts, but statements to this effect were made to me by more than one person who ought to have known the truth of the case, and whose veracity was above suspicion. When in pursuit of elephants or bison, very dark shikar clothes should be worn, the ordinary khaki colour being much too light for the jungles frequented by them. A friend of mine, who was wearing a light-coloured coat, once had a very narrow escape from a rogue elephant in the Billiga Rungam Hills, which he had fired at and knocked down; the brute got up again, and, seeing his light clothing, gave chase, and very nearly caught him.

When bolting from an elephant, endeavour to blink him by turning sharply off, down wind if possible. If in bamboo jungle, it is not difficult to dodge him, but he will catch you within twenty yards if you get into ground where there is undergrowth, which he will brush through like cobweb, while you are struggling in it with difficulty. The late Major Gordon Cumming had a theory that, by laming an elephant with a shot in the foot, he could be killed with greater certainty than by risking the usual head shots, which in heavy jungle result in many animals escaping badly wounded, owing to the difficulty usually experienced in hitting the brain. He told me that one day, in the Sacrabyle jungles, he had followed up a herd, and found the tusker under a tree, standing on three legs, in the way they are in the habit of doing while thus resting in shady spots. He could not get a favourable position for a head shot, so crept up and fired into the sole of one of the hind feet, which was raised from the ground. The poor brute turned round and attempted to charge, but was dead lame, and the hunter had no difficulty in giving him a quietus.

At first sight this appears a cruel method to adopt, but, considering the large percentage of wounded elephants that escape to suffer prolonged torture, it is probably more humane than the ordinary plan. In addition to selecting the usual tree of refuge near the firing point, it is very desirable to scan the surroundings, to decide on lines of retreat, free from impediments such as bushes, long grass, and creepers, in case of having to make a bolt of it with an empty rifle, a contingency that sooner or later is bound to occur when elephant shooting. To harden leaden bullets for elephants two ladles are required, one of which must be considerably smaller than the other; into the smaller one pour enough molten lead to make three bullets, add one-tenth of quicksilver, and stir with a bit of iron, so as to mix it well, then cast the bullets without loss of time. If the quicksilver was added to the molten lead in the larger ladle, it would evaporate too quickly. Tin is also used to harden bullets, but, being lighter than mercury, it lessens their penetration, and is therefore less efficacious. There is no sport that can be compared to tackling a solitary tusker, except, perhaps, following up a wounded tiger on foot. In shooting tigers from trees, or from a howdah, there is but little if any danger. The charge of a wounded bison can be stopped or turned by even a badly placed bullet; dangerous though he be, the size of a panther engenders a certain amount of contempt for him; a bear is not a very formidable opponent, although a plucky one as a rule; but in the case of a tusker the fight is a fairer one. Your heavy rifle feels uncommonly light in your hands as you approach him, and study his vast proportions, and you know that on it alone you must depend, and that if he is not killed the first shot, the odds are pretty evenly balanced between you.

After a victorious fight, you will, however, regret to see your huge antagonist lying dead, his feet and tusks the only portions of his immense frame that can be utilised. One always feels these pangs of remorse after the closing scene with all animals except tigers or panthers.

The largest tusker ever obtained in Southern India, was shot by Sir Victor Brooke and General Douglas

Hamilton, many years ago, at the southern extremity of the Billiga Rungam Hills, near Hassanoor. I remember hearing the story at Bangalore not very long after the occurrence. The tusker was with a herd, and both sportsmen fired at and wounded him very severely, but he recovered himself and went off for many miles. General Hamilton — who was an experienced shikari — was of opinion that this stern chase was a useless one; but, in deference to Sir Victor's entreaties, he accompanied him in the pursuit, and at length they sighted the tusker standing in a nullah, where Brooke knocked him over with a shot in the ear, eventually giving him another shot in the head as a *coup de grace*.

He was reported to have been eleven feet in height, and his best tusk measured about eight feet, the other was diseased, and was not a good specimen. It was a great piece of luck to get this splendid animal after the failure of the preliminary attack—such cases being very rare with elephants. He was probably a very old beast with a hardened skull, which may have stopped some of the bullets which would have been fatal to a younger animal. This tale proves the value of perseverance when shikaring—in no class of sport is this more necessary, than when in pursuit of wild elephants.

SPEARING A WOUNDED ANTELOPE.

CHAPTER XIII.

DEER (*CERVIDÆ*) AND ANTELOPES.

The Sambur—Description of—Stalking and driving the—Dogs useful in—Fondness for cinchona—Neddiwuttum—Successful stalk—Gopaulswamy Hill—Brahmin priests—Tippicado—Muddoor—Get a right and left—Unexpected result—Antler wounds—Sambur and wild dogs—Nilghai—Spotted deer—Muntjack deer—Barking powers of—Venison of—Four-horned antelope—The black buck—Stalking the—Spearing when wounded—Catching with hunting leopards—Ring-horned antelope—Mountain antelope—Mouse deer Burmese deer—Daray—Effect of Express bullet—Shedding of antlers.

THE trees composing the jungles in the Madras Presidency are mostly deciduous, shedding their leaves about the middle of March, when the weather begins to get very hot. For several months after this happens stalking cannot be attempted with any hope of success, owing to the noise made by the dead leaves when trodden upon; moreover, the annual grass burnings will have driven deer to moister localities, together with nobler game, to whose pursuit the sportsman is more likely to devote himself. The stalking season, therefore, may be said to be closed from the middle of March to the burst of the monsoon in June.

The sambur (C. Aristotelis) is the finest specimen of the deer tribe that roams the Southern Indian forests—a good stag standing fourteen hands at the shoulder, and weighing considerably more than any red deer of the Highlands of Scotland.* He is to be found in all wooded parts of the low country, preferring undulating or hilly ground, and on all the higher hills of the Western Ghauts, Neilgherries, Pulneys, and Annamullays, and it is on the grassy slopes of these ranges that he may best be stalked, which is the most sporting way of securing him. Unfortunately, however, this sport is confined to the few hours immediately after sunrise, and from 4 p.m. to sunset. On being wounded, or alarmed, he at once makes for one of the numerous sholahs, which are generally within a mile, and thus ends the stalk for that day, so far as he is concerned, and in this respect it differs from, and falls short of, the sport of the Highlands. He may also be tracked like bison, or be driven in closer jungles, but when this is attempted in the hill sholahs, dogs must be used on account of the dense cover. Driving for sambur has recently been prohibited on the Neilgherries, and it is to be hoped that this restriction may be extended to other districts, subject to certain reservations, such, for instance, as old hinds, crop-destruction, and meat supply for camp.

Old hinds are undesirable in many ways, and should be thinned out, as is the custom in Scotch deer forests.

* Viz., about forty stone.

My first experience of sambur shooting was at Kulhatty, on the Baba Booden Hills, in April, 1870. We had a large party, who were enjoying the hospitality of Colonel Hay, the Deputy Commissioner of the district, and had a series of picnics, in combination with sambur driving, which was carried out in the sholahs, with beaters and a "bobbery" pack of dogs, the guns being posted on the outskirts. In the smaller sholahs we had very fair sport, but the larger woods ran down the slopes to the heavy forests at the foot of the hills, and the deer always beat us here. Our best day resulted in five sambur, out of which there was but one really good head, but at that time many stags are in velvet. These hills are about 5000 feet above the sea; and although the days were very hot, even with a breeze,—the nights were delightfully cool. Further down the hills at Santawerry we also got an occasional sambur, when driving the coffee plantations and adjacent jungles for spotted deer and jungle sheep.

On the Neilgherries, in May, 1881, we (a party of three) made a trip from Wellington to the Orange Valley and Peerput Mund, commencing each day by stalking from five to nine o'clock in the morning. After breakfast the neighbouring sholahs were beaten for sambur, jungle sheep, and pigs, the latter being in an impossible country for the spear. Hinds were very numerous, but were not fired at. Stags were few and far between, and seldom seen when beating, although occasionally met with during the early morning stalks; Captain Croker, of my regiment, a good all-round sportsman, and one of the best snipe shots I ever saw, getting a fine stag his first morning. We had a motley crew of camp followers and hangers-on of sorts, from dog boys to bandy wallahs (bullock men), who clamoured for meat, and we got a mixed bag, which satiated them, and converted the camp into a species of shambles. No other beaters were obtainable, the Todahs (a hill tribe) being scarce in those parts, and our beaters were useless, after the second day, owing to their gourmandising propensities. My friends had then to return to Coonoor, but I spent two days beating the Orange Valley * sholahs, for a tiger which had been killing buffaloes, only meeting with a small stag. These sholahs were smaller than those at higher levels, and, by a judicious system of stops, could be managed fairly well by one gun. The headman of the Todahs came into camp at Koktal Mund on the second evening to report that the tiger had been poisoned by a sahib, who shall be nameless, only a few days before. I then went on to Ootacamund, and thence to Neddiwattum, as the guest of the hospitable and genial Bob Jagoe, who had a charming bungalow near the Government cinchona plantations; my colonel was also of the party, and we had a very pleasant time. The sambur, being very fond of the bark of the cinchona trees, were in the habit of jumping the fences, some six feet high, and, after luxuriating in the inclosures all night, returning to the sholahs in the early morning. It was impossible to intercept them, as they were clever enough to retrace their steps long before daylight. We beat the sholahs one day, but they were, as a rule, too thick for the beaters to penetrate, although they put out one good stag from a small sholah, which was hard hit, but escaped to the low country. I had, however, some nice stalks in the mornings and evenings. One morning, on peeping over a ridge, I saw two stags—a large and a small one—feeding towards a sholah on my left; they were some six hundred

* So called from the abundance of wild orange trees which adorn its slopes. The scarlet rhododendron is also prevalent.

yards out in the open, and were much on the alert, as an odious black monkey was hooting vigorously at me from an adjacent tree. Having tried the wind, it became evident that they would get it on arriving within two hundred yards of the sholah; we had therefore to intercept them before they reached that point.

The intervening ground was studded with a few large stones, and sloped gently down for about four hundred yards; but if a spot some two hundred and fifty yards in that direction could be reached unseen, we would be within a long shot of them by the time they got our wind.

Crossing the top of the ridge—which was their sky-line—when their heads were down, I got into the "back position" on the slope; and watching my opportunities, and pushing the rifle alongside foot by foot, reached the first stone safely, which was half-way to my objective point. The abominable monkey now became more demonstrative, shaking the boughs and swearing at me,* and the stags trotted forward a short distance and stopped, looking hard in my direction, but soon recommenced feeding and trying the red deer dodge of putting down their heads as if to graze, and then raising them sharply to see if anything was moving. I remained motionless during these agonising moments. Proceeding in this way, I at length got within two hundred yards, and as they might now wind me at any moment and gallop off, giving a difficult shot, I reversed my position and fired at the big stag. The bullet went over his back, but he did not stir for a few seconds, till the shot from the left barrel—aimed

* We subsequently found the fresh tracks of a tiger, which had evidently retired into the sholah on our approach, and the monkey's threats may have been intended for him.

lower—caught him in the neck and rolled him over dead. I paced the distance and found it to be 172 yards.

In the afternoon I had a long and unsuccessful stalk after another stag in undulating ground, where the wind perpetually shifting betrayed us in the end. The best sambur head I ever got was at the foot of Gopaulswamy Hill, a famous tract for all kinds of game, and which can be worked by camping on, or near the top of, the hill, which is 4500 feet above the level of the sea, thus avoiding the deadly malaria of the lower jungles. My camp was pitched on a coll joining the two highest points of the range, and close to a shrine dedicated to the Hindoo Pan, the shepherd's god, Gopaul. Some Brahmin priests who lived there paid me a visit soon after my arrival, imploring me to prohibit my Madrassee servants—who were pariahs—from drawing water from an adjacent holy well, and, on being asked how cooking and washing water was to be obtained, replied that if I drew the water myself all would be well, but that the low caste natives would defile it, and draw down the fury of Gopaul on all concerned. Their wishes were of course yielded to. They subsequently informed me that a sahib who had encamped there once before, had not restrained his servants, who desecrated the well. His tent was first blown down, and a severe domestic affliction befell him soon afterwards. A friend of mine informed me that these statements were not without foundation. From here one could command the jungles from Muddoor on the west, to Tippicado on the south, which were at one time perhaps the best in Southern India for elephants and bison, but notoriously unhealthy. The pull up the hill at the end of a long day, although very stiff work, was the only way to escape the malaria.

On one occasion, when following a rogue elephant at

Tippicado, I paid the travellers' bungalow there a visit, and found everybody down with fever, and a notice posted up recommending travellers not to stop the night there. Death was in the air, and the warning was respected. The Muddoor jungle is not so deadly when the ground has been well soaked by the monsoon about the beginning of July, but sambur are then in velvet; indeed, in these jungles, or the Annamullays, sambur were never shot by me except when required for the camp. In the latter forest they were fairly numerous, and in some cases absurdly tame, never having seen a human being before. I remember coming suddenly on a sambur stag when tracking bison one day; he bucked and snorted across the glade for twenty yards or so, and then turned round to gaze at the curious looking biped in shikar clothes; he then repeated the performance, and disappeared in the covert. Pigs on these occasions, too, gave much trouble, being full of curiosity, and distinctly hostile in manner; and with old boars it was awkward work, as one did not wish to disturb the forest by firing.

One evening, in the Annamullays, returning from Coochmullay, Ibex Hill, we came to the edge of a glade in the forest, and, peeping through some bamboos, saw two stag sambur within easy range.

The Carders, pathetically patting their stomachs, pointed at them to signify they wanted meat, so I fired right and left. Much to my surprise, the second stag bounded away apparently unhurt; but, on going up to the spot where he had been standing, I found a hind expiring in the long grass. She had been standing alongside the stag, between him and me, his antlers showing above her head, and her body thus intercepted the bullet intended for him. On approaching the stag, which was also dying, he kicked out,

SAMBUR AND WILD DOGS.

just grazing my leg, therefore one should look out for heels as well as horns of a wounded stag. The wounds caused by the latter are supposed never to heal, a superstition of long standing, as according to the old English rhyme:

From tooth of wolf or tusk of boar there is not much to fear,
But bad the smart from horn of hart, 'twill bring thee to thy bier.

In front of the bungalow at Toonacudavoo a stream ran over a cliff, forming a waterfall some thirty feet high. This was a favourite refuge for sambur when hunted by the wild dogs, which were numerous in the surrounding forests. The base of the cliff, being hollowed out by the action of the water, which also formed a deep pool in front, an admirable stronghold existed, protected in rear by the cliff itself, and in front by the falling water and pool. Here sambur were frequently brought to bay, the event being preceded by much "belling" in the neighbouring covert, the dogs, however, running mute on these occasions. The rifle was only used to protect the deer from its assailants. In the Nizam's dominions the sambur is to be found in most of the wooded districts. They, like other deer, are fond of the flower of the mhowa tree, and flock to the jungles containing it in the month of March, and are to be seen in herds of about a dozen or so, in the Parudi and Pakhal districts. The venison is very like tender beef, the tongue and marrow bones being considered great delicacies. The next animal on the list is the nilghai,* an antelope of semi-bovine build, and about the height of the sambur, but bulkier in make. He is essentially a low country animal, and resorts to the same wooded districts as the sambur, but is easier to stalk than that wary animal. I have never seen the nilghai in any part of Mysore, but they

* Portax picta.

are fairly numerous in the Nirmul and Pakhal districts of the Nizam's dominions. The bulls are about 14½ hands at the shoulder, the fore legs are comparatively short, and the weight should be 600lb. They are of a slatey blue colour, with dark mane, and a tuft of hair hangs from the throat, the face being brownish; smooth horns, less than 9 inches long, and a dewlap; the skin of which is very thick, and used for shields. He is more of an ox than an antelope, the females are of a reddish brown colour, and smaller than the males, the flesh is indifferent, but the tongue and marrow bones are esteemed as delicacies. A solitary bull is worth stalking, but on the whole not much sport is afforded by this animal.

They may sometimes be found in rideable country, or may be driven to it and speared, but such an opportunity never occurred to me. The axis, spotted deer or cheetul, is essentially a deer of the woods, never being seen in the maidān country, except in the vicinity of jungle. They prefer park-like forest near water, studded with thick clumps of jungle, and are not to be found above 4000 feet elevation. The lower slopes of the Southern Indian hills is the ground *par excellence* for them, and here they may be stalked without much difficulty, provided attention be given to the wind. With this deer, driving is better sport than stalking, and at Santawerry we often got sambur and jungle sheep, as well as spotted deer, on such occasions. Panthers, too, were sometimes turned out, and in some of the beats a gun loaded with No. 3 shot was used for the jungle and spur fowl which abounded there. It was a more suitable weapon than a 12-bore rifle for jungle sheep and mouse deer, so the custom was to load with ball cartridge at the commencement of the beats, when the larger animals were generally on foot, substituting the shot cartridges later on. One of the finest cheetul stags I ever got was driven out of a small patch of coffee within ten yards of me, and killed with No. 3 shot. Near the same spot, a few days before, I got two jungle sheep and a mouse deer in the same way, the gun on my left getting a sambur stag. Except when beating over a hill we generally employed only a dozen beaters and five dogs—pariahs of sorts—and found it ample, the most likely parts of the jungles being narrow strips at the bottom of the valleys, which could be easily commanded by four guns, two being in front and one on each flank. At Yemadoody, near the foot of these hills, Patterson and I found ourselves in a valley swarming with cheetul, and had some nice stalking in the early mornings, and two days' beating, entailing a large expenditure of ammunition, as the covert was thick and it was regular snap shooting. On the second day we were joined by two friends, who rode down from Santawerry for breakfast. We beat a more open tract of jungle near a lake, for three hours, and got five cheetul. The meat came in useful for the coolies on the coffee plantation belonging to our friends, and some of the heads were handsome trophies. Out of many stags shot by me the head of the last was the best, the horns being about thirty inches long. It was at the end of a long day, during which I had marched from Muddoor to Bandipore, thence to a ridge some two miles to the south of the bungalow, a favourite hunting ground of mine, and where it was reported that a family of four tigers had taken up their quarters, and were killing a number of cattle in the herds which were grazing in the neighbourhood. I visited one of the kills, and followed the tracks of the tigers (two) along a sandy nullah, where they had stopped to drink in some puddles, which were covered with small blue butterflies, and were consequently full of decaying organic matter, but after an hour the tracks led away from home, so we gave it up.

On the way home we started a herd of cheetul, headed by a stag, which dashed away, but halted again a few hundred yards off, croaking vigorously. Detaching my Koorumber shikari to distract their attention, I got to within ninety yards of the stag; he was end on to me, and the light was bad, but a lucky shot with the Express hit him in the haunch (the "usual place!"), this paralysed him, and running up I finished him with another shot. The remainder of the herd would hardly leave their fallen leader, and kept within twenty yards of him until I ran forward. It soon became pitch dark, the jungle was very thorny, and although not more than three miles from the bungalow, we took two hours to get back. The skin of the spotted deer is very handsome, rather larger than the fallow deer and glossier, and more richly coloured, the white spots showing better against the rich brown hide; the horns are not palmated, and I have never seen them with more than six points. The rib-faced, barking, or muntjac deer,* also known as the jungle sheep, prefers hilly ground covered with thick jungle, at not less than 1500 feet elevation; they are numerous on all southern Indian hills, being found in thick brushwood and dense sholahs up to 7500 feet elevation.

They do not exceed twenty inches in height, and are of a light red colour. For so small an animal they bark very loudly, much louder than the cheetul, when alarmed, making the jungles resound by day or night. The male is provided with two short, sharp tusks in the upper jaw. If broadside on, a gun loaded with No. 3 shot will kill them

* C. muntjac.

up to thirty yards; they have a habit of squatting like a rabbit, and will then let you pass within a few yards without moving, often starting up behind, within range, after you have passed on. The venison is much appreciated, and is supposed to be only inferior to that of the mouse deer. The four-horned antelope * resembles the muntjac in size and shape, but is lighter in colour, nor does it frequent such high altitudes. The buck is provided with four horns, the frontals being less than one inch in length, the posterior ones over four inches. A perfect specimen is very rare, and on the whole they are much scarcer than either the muntjac or chikāra. I once got a fair specimen in the Bandipore jungle, in the country towards Gundulpett. The chikāra,† or ravine deer, is found in undulating country, covered with scrub jungle and intersected by ravines and nullahs; they are graceful little creatures, of a light chesnut colour, with white neck; both sexes have horns, those of the doe being small and smooth. In open spaces in scrub jungle, collections of droppings will often be observed arranged on the circumference of a circle of about 6ft. in diameter, the shikaris assert that these deposits are formed by chikāra, which form up thus—heads facing outwards—to keep watch on all sides.

The black buck‡ is the most beautiful of all antelopes, and affords better sport than any of the other species found in India. He stands over seven hands high, and weighs about six stone. The bucks are very dark brown all over except on the belly, throat, and about the face, which are more or less white. As they get older the coat becomes darker by degrees until they arrive at the age of six years, when it is almost black.

* Tetraceros quadricornis. † Gazelle Bennetti.

‡ Antelope Bezoartica.

In Southern India their horns seldom exceed eighteen inches in length, but I have shot one with twenty inch horns, and in Northern India they are not uncommonly found with horns from four to six inches longer. The does are hornless, uninteresting-looking animals, of a yellowish colour marked with white.

This antelope is always found in maidān country in herds of from six to sixty, and its favourite haunts are large plains interspersed with tracts of scrub jungle, and bordered by cultivated land, such as cholum fields—which they raid during the night.

A few years ago antelope were plentiful near Sarjapoor and Kulhulli, some thirty miles south-east of Bangalore, in good stalking ground, the country being undulating, and dotted with isolated clumps of bajr shrubs, &c.; in this district, too, some good snipe grounds existed, where, with good luck and straight powder, bags of thirty couple were obtainable. The usual programme was to dawk from Bangalore during the night, so as to be on the antelope ground at daylight, then to stalk until breakfast time, about 9 A.M., devoting the rest of the day to snipe, which lay better when the sun was hot. One morning at Kulhully, I had been ineffectually stalking a small herd of antelope for nearly two hours, when some natives came up, suggesting that they should drive them for me. The neighbouring cholum crops had suffered much from their depredations, and the ryots* were particularly keen on getting them killed. At the opposite side of the main road to Bangalore, was a large open plain fringed by cultivated land, towards which the herd would probably make, so I posted myself to intercept them as they crossed the road. They first headed towards the upper end of a

* Cultivators.

large tank, about a quarter of a mile to my left front, as I faced the beat, but the right wing of the beaters worked round through some bajree (cholum-millet) fields, and turned them back, the centre and left then advancing, drove them into some swampy ground at the edges of the tank, where three does became hopelessly bogged, and were killed by the beaters, the remaining six, charging the line, broke back.

To the east of Bangalore near some casuarina plantations at Maloor, some nice stalking was also to be had, while, to the west, in the Chittledroog district, the vast plains contained many herds, and further south near Hassan, the main road to Bangalore ran through excellent ground, where, by screening oneself with a bullock cart shots could be obtained at half a dozen bucks in a few hours.

In stalking a herd of antelope without the aid of a cart, which can often be done in rough ground, the sportsman should always shape his course towards the head of the herd, if possible.

My favourite plan was to stalk them with my horse, which was led by the syce carrying a spear, while I endeavoured to make myself as unconspicuous as possible, by keeping step with the horse, and marching close to him on the side remote from the herd, usually getting within 150 yards, when aim was taken from the knee, the syce and horse continuing to move on to divert their attention from me. If one was wounded the horse and spear were available for a gallop, everything of course depended on the position of the wound, and the buck usually collapsed within a mile; but on one occasion, at Cadoor, I had a rattling gallop of over three miles, before getting within spearing distance. Near Hyderabad (Deccan) they were often killed by tame hunting leopards, which were taken out on bullock carts driven by natives. When within 150 yards of the buck, the leopard was loosed and unhooded, and usually overtook and killed his quarry within a few hundred yards. It seldom exceeded 300 yards when pursuing, and if unsuccessful, it would squat down and sulk. This ground, named the Rumnah* was preserved by the Nizam chiefly for this sport, and numerous herds existed there, some stray bucks from which often crossed the march into the Mowl Ali country, and afforded sport to the officers quartered at Trimulgherry. The maidān country about Beder and Kondelwaddy was also frequented by antelope, and I once saw a herd of about one hundred at the latter place. At Chamrajnuggar, near the scene of Saunderson's Keddah operations, there was a variety named the ring-horned antelope, of which, with much difficulty, I secured a specimen—a fair buck, but not the best one of the herd, which consisted of seven individuals.† The mountain antelope, a rare variety, exists on the Neilgherry and Pulney hills. I never met one, but heard of two near Pykara; it is said to resemble a doe antelope in size and colour, but has a longer coat, and is provided with very short and sharp horns. The mouse deer is a pretty little creature, about the size of a hare, of an olive colour with a yellow stripe and markings along each side. They are found in the Mysore and Annamullay forests, and are not at all uncommon. In Burmah, the theming or brow-antlered deer, is found in the large plains, lying near the Setang river. They are by no means plentiful, and, owing

* Lands on which the grass is allowed to grow long for thatching, &c.

† I think it must have been a large chikāra, the horns being very similar to those of that antelope.

to the flat open ground they frequent, are difficult to stalk. Driving is usually resorted to, the preliminary stalking operations having failed. The best specimen I ever saw was shot by Captain Croker of my regiment, on an occasion when we were both nearly bagged by one of the sportsmen, who enfiladed the line of guns. On that memorable day we got a stag and a hind, both fine animals, nearly as large as red deer, but lighter in colour. The venison tasted like goose. I have a good head now in my possession, which was shot sometime after in the same tract.

The daray, also a Burmese deer, much resembling a roe, were very abundant in the large grassy plains thereabouts. They were invariably driven by beaters and dogs, the sport being a combination of coursing and shooting and not of a particularly exciting description.

The first shot I ever fired with an Express rifle was at one of these small deer not sixty yards off, a particularly small one he was too. The bullet struck him in the neck, none of the fragments emerging on the opposite side, although there was not more than 3½ inches to be penetrated. This was with a ·500 rifle, and its performance made me sceptical about its powers if used against dangerous game.

It is very doubtful whether the older sambur stags shed their horns annually. Some sportsmen assert that they do so; others that it only occurs every third year. A sambur stag is not fully developed till he has reached the age of eight years. His antlers then are very massive, and it is unlikely that the reproduction of so much bony tissue should be thrown every year on the animal's system.

The horns are at their best in the cold weather, and at that time I have never met a sambur stag in velvet; but the spotted deer seem to have no fixed season for shedding theirs, individuals being found in velvet throughout the year, with perhaps the exception of the months of January and February, when I have never had an opportunity of shooting one, and can therefore make no statement on the subject.

IBEX GROUND.

CHAPTER XIV.

THE IBEX (*Capra Warryato*)

Ibex on Neilgherries and Pulneys—Cause of decrease—Description of—Annamullay ibex hills—Coochmullay—"Desperation Chasm"—Unsuccessful stalk—Shoot two sambur—Pig's nest—Perringoondah Mullay—Difficulties *en route*—Fresh tracks of elephants—The shooting ground—Kill a saddle back—Demoralised Carders—Shoot another buck—Find a herd—Shoot two bucks and a doe—Get a right and left—Lose both animals over precipice—Awkward predicament—Cobra—Leeches—Measurement of ibex—Return to Toonacudavoo—Subsequently revisit hill—Tiger—Ibex in Scinde—Ibex ground near Goodaloor—Scarcity of ibex—Numerous on Annamullays—Stalking tactics.

In former years this animal, the wild goat of the Neilgherries—was plentiful in certain favoured localities on those hills and the Pulneys, but since the influx of tea and coffee planters, and the gradually increasing crowd of hot weather visitors from the plains, many of whom are keen sportsmen, these unfortunate animals have been persistently persecuted, and greatly reduced in numbers.

This chapter will be confined to the pursuit of the ibex of the Annamullays, for, although I have stalked on some of the Neilgherry ibex hills, the vicissitudes of the chase invariably brought sambur on the *tapis*, and I could not resist following that fine animal instead. The ibex of the Annamullays is precisely the same animal as that of the Neilgherries and Pulneys; a good buck stands about ten hands high at the shoulder, and is a strongly built, heavy animal, but as active as a monkey; the horns are curved and about fourteen inches long. As he grows old the hair on his back becomes light in colour, and that on the flanks darkens, the contrast forming a mark like a saddle, which catches the eye at once, so that there is no difficulty in picking out the old bucks. There were four ibex hills within reach of my headquarters at Toonacudavoo in the Annamullays, the first and worst was about seven miles off, near Poolakul, and was but seldom frequented by them, being merely a refuge in bad weather, or when they had been shot at elsewhere, or hunted by panthers —their mortal enemies.

There were two hills at Coochmullay, some ten miles off. These could be shot from Toonacudavoo by starting early and returning late; it was a real hard day's work, but generally worth the trouble. The last and best hill was named Perringoondah Mullay, which, being interpreted, means "the hill of the fruit track" or "pass." Partly on account of the distance and partly of the intervening rivers and nature of the jungle, it was necessary to camp here the previous night; the hill itself, too, was large and required some hours' work to do it justice. As the track led through part of the forest much frequented by bison, the day of the march there was not always a blank one.

My first day with ibex was at Coochmullay. Starting early we called at a Mulser village on the way for a couple of coolies. The Mulsers are a jungle tribe that live on the lower slopes of the hills, and are looked down upon, literally and figuratively, by the Carders. A stiff pull for two hours landed us on the plateau of the first hill. We had suffered severely from the leeches which swarmed in some parts of the jungles at the foot of the hills, and, in spite of every precaution, had found their way to all the tender parts of our frames. So after picking off all the marauders, we searched round the hill most carefully, but saw no ibex, although we found their fresh tracks in several places. The plateau of the second hill was at a higher level, and separated from the one we were on, by a very ugly chasm, only a few feet in breadth, but the opposite bank was a mere ledge at the foot of a steep cliff. It was, moreover, at least a foot higher than the take off, and a false step would result in a sheer descent of several thousand feet down to the low country, as this spot was on an overhanging cliff. The Carders gave me a lead over. They were as active as cats, and, as there was not room on the narrow ledge for more than one person, they scaled the opposing cliff; and hauled me up the face of it with ropes they had brought for the purpose.

The view from this higher plateau was magnificent, the primeval forest, nearly 6000 feet below, resembling a vast green sward, streaked by silver threads, such being the appearance of the rivers from that distance, while far away to the north the blue peaks of the Neilgherries formed a picturesque background.

A thickish mist now began to drive across the hill, but soon finding fresh traces, Atlay and I pushed on. At length he pointed out three ibex, much larger animals than I expected, being about the size of dhobies'* donkeys.

They were about 150 yards off—a rather difficult shot, and as a strong wind was blowing, I knelt down to get a steadier aim, but uttering a shrill whistle, they bounded away before the sights could be aligned—and believing more were close at hand I did not risk the shot. We followed them round the hill, recrossing "Desperation Chasm"—an odious experience—to the lower plateau, but they were very wary, and after stalking them for an hour they took refuge in a sholah, where it was useless to follow them, so we dejectedly faced homewards, as the sun was getting low, and the journey before us a long one. On the way we shot two sambur, and found a huge pig's nest, as usual situated in the middle of a thick clump of the hill gooseberry, which almost excluded daylight. The structure consisted of small branches piled up two feet high, and covering a space fully twenty yards square. Atlay was adverse to exploring it, but I insisted on doing so, but found the family "not at home." These curious constructions are to be found in all the larger jungles infested by wild pigs in the Mysore country, but I have never seen them in those of the Nizam's dominions.

My next expedition after ibex, four days later on, was more successful. Owing to heavy and continued rains the watercourses were much swollen, even the smaller ones being waist-deep, but after an arduous march of six hours,

* Washerman.

we arrived at two o'clock one afternoon at the foot of the Perringoondah Mullay ibex hill, and set to work to light a fire, while two of the Carders constructed a small but comfortable little hut, of bamboo framework, covered by leaves of the wild plaintain and tree fern, but lighting a fire was a more difficult matter. It was raining heavily, and everything was drenched; the heads came off the matches, so we had recourse to flint and steel. At length, after an hour of dexterous manipulation, this was accomplished. Then they cut some bundles of long lemon grass for my bed; it was swarming with leeches, but by holding it in the smoke of the fire we got rid of the majority—some, however, remaining, as I discovered when I turned in for the night.

The place selected for the camp was in a small natural clearing on an under feature of the Ibex Hill, the ground on each side sloping steeply away. A herd of wild elephants had been foraging there, a few hours before our arrival, and I was surprised to find their tracks in places that seemed impassable for such ponderous creatures.

We started early next morning up the slope of the hill, and, after a mile of steep clambering, reached the edge of the shooting ground, a long grassy slope with patches of coarse fern and brackens, interspersed with outcrops of rock. The upper slopes were barer and rockier, the summit being enveloped in dense fog, which cleared now and then for a few minutes when the wind blew strongly. It was what I once heard a ghillie term "level climbing," *i.e.*, a slope of about five degrees. Atlay and his companion soon began to exhibit the effects of wet and cold, which seem to stupify all natives, whether of the hills or plains; the former was leading, and we had only proceeded a few hundred yards, when a grand saddle-back sprang up about eighty yards ahead, unseen by him. I told him to lie down, but he did not hear me, his head and ears being covered with a cumbley (blanket). Luckily the buck stopped to gaze at us for a few seconds, so, stepping aside, I fired, and heard the bullet strike. Atlay fell down with fright, believing he was shot, and the buck bounded off, apparently unhurt, and disappeared over some rising ground in front. We followed his tracks some distance, finding no sign of blood, but found him lying dead about three hundred yards away at the foot of a small declivity. The bullet had passed through the lungs in front of the heart. This was the best buck I ever shot, a real old solitary saddle-back—the solitary ones being generally good specimens. As we gradually progressed up the hill, the mist became thicker, and the shikaries correspondingly useless from the cold, so I went on ahead, and presently a puff of wind blew the fog aside and disclosed three ibex within forty yards. They were moving slowly down the slope, and suddenly disappeared from view in a hollow, but quickly emerged on the opposite slope and stood for a few seconds. Selecting the largest, a handsome buck, I fired, and over he rolled, apparently quite dead, down the slope. I ran after him for a short distance, but was stopped by warning shouts from Atlay. The body continued to roll down, and, gaining impetus as it descended, cannoned from rock to rock, finally vanishing over the edge of a precipice into a sholah 200 feet below. The Carders said they would get him next day, so we continued the ascent towards the summit.

About half a mile farther on, I peeped over the edge of a cliff, and discovered a herd of fifteen ibex about fifty yards off, on a ledge of rock enveloped in mist, and was lucky enough to kill the largest buck with my right barrel, but missed another buck with my left, the remainder ran a few yards and halted, not knowing whence the danger came, and evidently bewildered, as I was above them, and they kept looking everywhere except in that direction. Creeping forward I got a buck and a doe right and left, and had time to reload and fire a snap-shot at another buck as he bounded off with the rest of the herd, but missed him. They then disappeared into the mist, bounding from crag to crag in a marvellous way. The shikaries begged for one more ibex for their village, and as I knew there were at least two very good bucks in front, being the ones I had missed, on we went.

The herd had not gone more than a few hundred yards, and we soon came upon them again, and I knocked over two bucks, right and left, which were standing close to each other on a pinnacle enveloped in fog. Atlay said we should not be able to get them. I got close to the spot, and found they had fallen over a precipice into a forest at the foot of the hill, far, far below. Atlay explained that it was impossible to reach them from where we were, even with ropes, but that it could be done from our encampment, or from one of their villages near Perrincudavoo, and that it would be a two days' job. This was very disheartening, but could not be helped. Returning to where the buck and doe had been shot, I climbed down the face of the precipice to recover them, and had no difficulty with the first one, which had fallen on a ledge just below the plateau, but the other was in a very difficult spot to reach on a sort of isolated pinnacle, the surroundings of which could not be ascertained, owing to the thick fog. The ledge on which the first one (a doe) had fallen, ran along the face of the cliff to within a few yards of the pinnacle, where the buck was stuck in a cleft, but then gradually got narrower. Along this I crept for some yards. The Carders could not help me; indeed they were utterly demoralised by cold and wet, and would not venture beyond where the doe fell. The mist now cleared away for a few seconds, and I found myself on a ledge barely a yard wide overhanging the low country. It was too narrow to turn round, and the only way out of the dilemma was to crawl backwards like a crab for some ten yards. This was accordingly done, but it was unpleasant work. The ledge then became wider, and it was easy going, but the buck had to be abandoned. While this performance was going on solitary members of the scattered herd would suddenly spring upon an adjacent peak, and after a good stare at me would again disappear into the mist with a shrill whistle.

The Carders being done—played out—and the sport having been good, I decided not to harry the hill any more that day, so sat down to smoke a pipe. Atlay presently pointed to a tuft of grass at my feet, and there was a cobra coiled up within a yard of me! I was surprised to see him at this elevation, but he was, like the Carders, torpid from the cold. When the pipe was finished I pulled three large hill leeches off my neck, quite different to the ordinary sholah leech, being ten times the size, so with all their advantages, these delightful hills are not without certain drawbacks. The first buck was the best of the lot; he measured as follows: height, 10½ hands; length from nose to tail, 6 feet 5 inches; girth, 4 feet 9 inches; length of horns, 14½ inches, 8 inches round base. We had a difficult march back to Toonacudavoo that afternoon through the leech jungles and swollen streams, not arriving till after dark. The Carders and camp servants were so heavily laden with ibex meat they could barely crawl along. They declared the meat of the bucks was the best for eating, being full of flavour, but the musky smell was too strong for me; the doe, however, was excellent. On subsequent occasions I revisited the ibex ground and explored the peak, as a rule having good sport, but losing some fine specimens over the precipices. One foggy day the whole hill was traversed without seeing a single ibex, but the cause was evident—a tiger had been before me, and his fresh pugs were visible in many places. When quartered at Kurrachee in 1869, ibex were reported to exist in the hills to the north-west of that station, but that it was useless to attempt shikaring there, owing to the jealousy of a Government official, whose myrmidons drove the hills in front of every unfortunate sahib who attempted to shoot on what the great man evidently considered his private preserve.

These ibex were quite different to the Southern Indian species, being akin to those of the Himalayas, but smaller. They are also considerably smaller than the Neilgherry animal, being only five feet in length and less than eight hands in height. Their horns, however, although similar in shape, are much more imposing, being nearly three feet long and thick in proportion.

The precipices overhanging the Goodaloor Pass—which is the ghaut leading westwards from Ootacamund to Cannanore, and which debouches into the Wynaad, near the village of Goodaloor—were in former years much frequented by ibex, as also were the high ranges lying to the south-west, and these were occasionally visited by them in the years 1880-81, but the herds were small and as wild as hawks, owing to the incessant harrying to which they had been subjected, which will certainly lead to their absolute extinction if persisted in, unless the Game

Laws since adopted and promulgated, save them from this fate.

In order to get good ibex shooting it was necessary to go further afield, to remoter districts—such, for instance, as the higher ranges of the Annamullays, that vast extent of unexplored and uninhabited highlands stretching away southwards into Travancore.

These ranges are difficult of access and quite unsuited to the operations of sybarites, and have only been visited by a few keen sportsmen, who did not mind roughing it, and running the risk of fever in the lower valleys, which must first be traversed in order to reach them. I had projected a trip to these happy hunting grounds, but was ordered home to the Depot, but my friend who went there, told me he saw herds of ibex numbering seventy individuals, which was probably an amalgamation of several smaller herds which had been attracted by better pasturage or been driven by stress of weather from the higher peaks.

He obtained seven good bucks, three bull bison, and a shot at a tusker during his last expedition, which extended for a period of six weeks.

The ibex stalker always endeavours to get above the herd, as they never seem to expect danger from this quarter, and the sentinel—which is always posted on the look out—devotes his attention to the ground lying on a level with, or below the herd. The sport is exciting in itself—apart from the dangerous nature of the ground on which it is carried out—the scenery is beautiful, the climate cool—considerable woodcraft is necessary to obtain a prize, and altogether it is one of the most enjoyable sports of Southern India.

CHAPTER XV.

MISCELLANEOUS.

Description of jungles—Annual burning of—Result as regards game—Hot weather best for tiger shooting—Water buffaloes for ties—Use of, with wounded tiger—Dhers—Gāras—Human victims—Maxims for the jungle—Cream-coloured tiger — Tiger's annual meat bill — Precautions when approaching a kill—Conduct if charged—Tracks of wounded animals—Heavy charges of powder—Village shikaris—Diplomacy necessary—Camp—Intelligence wallah—Food supply in remote spots—Evergreen trees—Climbing tigers—Duty on being posted—Tiger's larder—Tiger and boar—Charges of wounded tiger—Gallop after a wolf—Wild dogs—Native ideas of—Hyenas—Pythons—Adventure with—Cobras—Hamadryad—Bis cobra—Tarantula—Where to aim—Allowances to be made when aiming—Measurement of bison horns.

THE jungles of Southern India may be roughly classified under two headings, viz., tree and scrub jungles—the former being sub-divided into primeval or virgin forest, containing large timber trees, such as the teak, rosewood, and blackwood, of the Annamullays—and into ordinary tree jungle, consisting of banian, peepul, olibanum (salei) wood apple, mhowa, bastard teak, and trees as a rule not exceeding forty feet in height, such as are found in the majority of low-country wooded districts. Scrub jungles are mainly composed of bushes such as the jāmun, caroonda, bair, custard apple, and kino trees, generally not exceeding fifteen feet in height, but dotted here and there with trees of nobler growth. The term "jungle" signifies wild, waste, or uncultivated land, and embraces everything of the sort, from primeval forests down to grass rumnahs.* Before the middle of March all these tracts in the low country, which during the cold weather have afforded grazing for their cattle, are burnt by the villagers to get rid of the long and coarse grass, so as to ensure a young growth with the advent of the rains. The ashes caused by these burnings fertilise the soil, and in Burmah the rice fields are enriched by the ashes of the long straw, which is left standing with a similar object. The result of the conflagrations is to deprive the greater part of the country of cover for game of all kinds, which then betake themselves to areas which may have escaped the ordeal. Certain low-lying districts are annually exempted from burning, in order to afford grazing for immense herds of cattle collected from various villages and placed under charge of gowlees (herds) during the hot weather, who drive them to fresh fields and pastures new, as the grazing becomes exhausted in a given district.

A few so-called "mango showers" fall at intervals during the hot weather months of April and May, and the young grass soon begins to sprout, under their genial influence, in combination with the top dressing of ashes already furnished by the fires; but grazing is not in sufficient quantity to tempt the larger kinds of herbivorous game from their fastnesses before the middle of June. Therefore the hot weather months are those usually devoted to tiger shooting, as these animals, together with those they prey upon, cannot exist without water and shade, and have then to concentrate in the comparatively restricted areas which fulfil these requirements. The majority of the smaller tanks and nullahs throughout the country will

* Large expanses of meadow.

have become dried up before these months set in, and it is only in the bends of the larger nullahs that some pools will remain; here, too, will be found evergreen bushes, such as caroonda and jāmun, so that the two primary necessities of game—viz., covert and water—are available. Few tiger stories are read without some reference being made to a nullah; the above explanation is the solution of the problem, but many of the cattle-lifter type of tiger follow the migrations of the cattle herds, as already described, few flocks being free from parasites of this kind. The water buffaloes seldom accompany these flocks, as they can generally be watered and grazed in proximity to their villages; they are less valuable than the ordinary bail, and more easily obtainable for ties, but when in a herd, no tiger will venture near them, as they are very plucky animals, and when their blood is roused by the smell of a tiger, they will pursue him through any jungle, and are often used to oust a wounded tiger from his stronghold by being driven into it. The tiger does not, however, appreciate their beef as he does that of the ox, and he will often pass by tied-up haylas, and stalk and kill one of a herd of the ordinary oxen, as some of these also are retained in suitable localities which may exist near certain villages, even in the hot weather months. On these occasions, however, the kill is soon found out by the Dhers, and the sportsman on repairing to the spot will often find that they have eaten up whatever portion the tiger may have left after his preliminary meal.

The Dhers, also known as Bēgaris, are pariahs, or outcasts, who are not allowed to live in the villages, but are assigned some spot on their confines, and receive certain portions of land rent free, in return for which they are obliged to act as village scavengers, and as coolies or guides to travellers; they are, moreover, entitled to the carcases of all village animals that may die, or be killed by beasts of prey, and they are always on the watch for windfalls of this kind.

When a tiger kills a herd animal, the gowlees give information to the Dhers, who immediately sally forth and appropriate whatever remains of the carcase, and it is only in parts of the jungle remote from villages, that the sportsman has any chance of anticipating them.

Both tigers and panthers kill their prey with the large canine teeth, holding on to the neck and withers with their claws, the marks of which will always be visible.

If a tiger kills an animal rather late in the morning, when the sun is hot, after dragging the carcase to a shady spot, he will often lie up close by to watch it, and to prevent the vultures from eating it; indeed, he not unfrequently kills these birds when thus engaged. These late kills are, as a rule, made among herd oxen when grazing, and the first thing to be done is to stop the Dhers from interfering with them. The position of the kill will be indicated by the vultures circling over it, and if none of them appear to settle down; it is a strong inference that the tiger is there. Two courses are open: either to arrange for a beat at once, or to sit over the kill in a mechaun. The shikari will decide which is the better plan to adopt. If the tiger is "ringed," beating will be the best, otherwise the making of the mechaun should be proceeded with forthwith, so that it may be completed some hours before sunset, as it is of the utmost importance that the place should be perfectly quiet then. The selection of the tree for the mechaun will depend upon local circumstances, and the platform should be disguised by leafy branches, and be of small dimensions, viz., only large enough for the sahib and one shikari; moreover, the making of it should be conducted as noiselessly as possible. If water is in the vicinity the tiger will sometimes lie up near the kill until he has eaten it all. I remember getting news of a gāra on a Sunday evening, which had occurred the previous day; beaters were not then procurable, but next day, after a lapse of forty-eight hours, he was driven out from a patch of jungle close by.

After drinking the blood—if the sun is not high, as has been already stated—the tiger begins his meal at the hind quarters, but the panther prefers the flank, and works towards the stomach, being very partial to the liver. Thus one can see at a glance by which of these animals the gāra has been made. On his second visit—or sometimes when very hungry—the tiger extends his operations to flank, belly, and liver. It is strange that when a human being is the victim, the feet are usually the first portions demolished. The cannibals on the West Coast of Africa always commence with the hands and feet, and they probably know which are the best tit-bits. When in pursuit of big game never appear suddenly in a glade, nor over the top of a ridge, nor round a rocky corner or point of jungle. Many a shot is lost in this way. Always examine the ground in front before showing yourself. On such occasions observe your shikaries and jungle-wallahs, and imitate their movements. Adopt their cautious demeanour, even when proceeding along a path or track far from any spot where you expect to find game. You may depend upon it, that these born and bred jungle men, follow the best method of threading their native wilds. It is almost superfluous to add a warning against talking when on the look-out for game. When your tracker wishes to call attention, he imitates the chirp of a squirrel or cluck of a lizard, sounds well known in the jungle, and which are easily learned. When copied for a short time, this jungle demeanour becomes habitual, and ceases to be irksome. If any of your followers show the least disposition to cough when waiting for game—send them away forthwith. It is caused by fear, and will certainly break out afresh if the animal appears. On four occasions I lost shots by the coughing of my shikari before my experience was gained. On another occasion, a tiger was walking down a nullah straight towards a friend, who was posted on my right. His shikari began to funk and coughed, whereupon the tiger turned back, and, emerging within ten yards of me, was killed by a single spherical bullet from my rifle. After shooting a tiger, the body should not be permitted to lie upon hot stones or rocky ground, as the hair will subsequently fall off the skin at every point where it has been thus touched; nor is it wise to sit on the body of a dead tiger, for as it cools the ticks leave it, and will settle on the nearest living substitute. The pugs of a tiger are larger and rounder than those of a tigress, which are oval in shape, and not much larger than a bōr batcha's, from which, indeed, they are not easily distinguishable. The tigress has seldom more than three cubs at a birth, of which but two, as a rule, survive the first year. She then teaches them how to kill their prey, and they remain with her till they are two years old, being then generally sent off to shift for themselves. Occasionally a family party of tigers will be found in some favoured locality, whose younger members will be four years old at least, and will have been killing for themselves for more than two years. With good luck and proper management four, or even five, tigers may then be shot in one day.

Some years ago news was brought me of a white or cream coloured tiger being in a certain district, where, however, I never had an opportunity of shikaring him. He was reputed to be stripeless. As a tiger gets old, his stripes become faded, and less clear in outline, but this cream coloured one was reported, on good authority, to be absolutely devoid of any. The tiger kills at least once in every five days, so his bag for one year would amount to seventy-three head. Sixty of these would be cattle averaging fully twelve rupees each in value, so at a moderate computation, his annual bill for meat would reach seven hundred rupees—a heavy sum to be visited on poor villagers. In jungles that have been much shot over, tigers become suspicious, and will often decline to kill the tied-up animals, but by tying two or three within twenty yards of each other, so as to resemble a herd, he may often be induced to kill—his cunning, however, may then cause him to avoid lying up in the neighbourhood. If a tigress with cubs meets with these animals she will probably kill the lot, in order to teach her young ones their business, but as young water buffaloes only cost six rupees apiece, the outlay will not be very heavy. It has already been mentioned that a herd of buffaloes is often of service in driving a wounded tiger from some spot he may be lying up in; but if they are not forthcoming, a herd of oxen, or even of goats, may be used for the purpose—they will at all events often make him disclose his whereabouts.

When approaching a kill, rifles should be full cocked, and carried at the ready, and the most open ground selected for the advance. The tiger will almost invariably move off (if he happens to be there), but he may perhaps attempt to drive away the intruders by a hostile demonstration. The presence of two or more individuals is usually enough to force him to retire, but if he charges, every man must stand fast, and for this reason a gāra should never be approached except when along with thoroughly dependable men. A friend of mine was once charged by a tiger near Luchwalli, in Mysore, on visiting a gāra—the brute rushing out roaring, in the orthodox way, but he stood his ground, and the tiger changed his mind when within a few yards, and skulked off through some thick grass, which saved him—during his advance and retreat—from being fired at. When following up the pugs of a wounded tiger or panther, if the claw marks show that they have been driven deeply into the ground, it is a sure sign of his being severely wounded; and in the case of deer or bison, the separation of the hoofs, as shown by the slots, is a similar indication. When tracking up a wounded animal, do not be discouraged by the absence of blood, as owing to internal hæmorrhage the mortally wounded animal often shows no traces of it. When firing heavy charges, the jar often causes both barrels to go off simultaneously—a very unpleasant experience, which should be obviated by only full cocking one barrel at a time. When tiger shooting, the first thing to be done on arriving at a village is to enlist the services of the local native shikari at any price. He is always thoroughly acquainted with the numbers and habits of the tigers and other animals in the district, and is king of his own jungle. No shikar party is complete without a shikari to act in an administrative capacity, to elicit khabar, to obtain haylas and beaters, and to square the village shikaries—often a very difficult task, and one that requires the greatest tact, for as a rule they resent inroads by visitors, whose performances may dim their local reputations as tiger slayers, and they are reticent and obstinate to a degree. The points on which information is necessary may be briefly enumerated as follows:—Number of tigers, usual haunts, drinking places; when and where last gāra occurred; number of beaters obtainable; whether other sahibs have ever shot there, and with what results; whether any beaters were ever killed by a tiger; if any big game in addition to tigers frequent the jungle.

The Intelligence Department wallah must have at least one day's start of the party. This can always be arranged, for his duties as an executive shikari should be very light. By the time you arrive at the new camp he will have obtained some information on the above points; but, as the local man parts with his secrets slowly, you must be patient, as a few days will probably reveal everything that is required. To avoid bringing too much pressure on the food supplies of villages in remote districts, a large quantity of rice, fowls, &c., should be taken with the camp baggage. It is also desirable to purchase some young buffaloes, to march with the caravan, as in many places the people object to furnish animals for baits.

Natives say that the peepul tree affords the healthiest and coolest shade for a camp, but mango trees and banians are quite as good. The tamarind tree should be avoided, as it harbours ticks, as large as beans, and they bite malignantly. From the rustling of its leaves in the faintest breeze, the peepul tree soothes one with the idea that it is cool, perhaps the native opinion of its shade is attributable to this circumstance.

Since writing the chapter on tigers, an account in the *Field*, of the 7th April, 1894, has appeared, headed "Sport in the Nirmul Jungle," in which details are given of a tiger taking a man off a branch 20 feet 7 inches above the ground. The writer stated that this was not done by a spring, but by regular climbing up a difficult tree. Some years ago an account appeared in a Madras paper of a tiger having been shot in a tree in the Neilgherry hills, at an elevation of twenty feet above the ground. These cases must be considered very exceptional, and any ordinary wound ought to incapacitate the tiger from performing such feats either by climbing or springing.

On being posted, the first thing to do is to scan the adjacent jungle, to ascertain the passes by which the tiger is most likely to approach, and, if in a tree, to take up a position so that you can readily direct your fire on each.

In addition to cattle, the tiger also kills deer, wild pigs, porcupines, monkeys, and even pea fowl ; and when hard pressed by hunger, will eat frogs, and grub like the bear under stones and cattle droppings for the beetles that take refuge there.

Wild pigs are his favourite food and are more easily caught than deer, as they are in the habit of grubbing up the ground for roots, and while thus engaged are more easily stalked. The tiger will seldom tackle the old boar, who is too good a warrior for him, and sometimes worsts him in single combat.

In the hot weather trips made by the sportsmen from Secunderabad, one or more instances happened from time to time, of wounded tigers charging those who were following them up ; but an accident never occurred on these rather ticklish occasions, as the brute was invariably shot dead or turned by the fire of the group, every man of which invariably stood firm ; all the same, there were some narrow shaves, the wounded tiger often only swerving at the last moment, and passing within a few feet of the group of sportsmen. Under similar circumstances, a panther would probably charge home, as he is a much more courageous animal, although inferior to the tiger in power of jaw and claw. The village shikari invariably shoots his tiger either over water or over a kill, and in the latter case he takes care to be at least twenty feet from the ground, and in the bad light often misses or wounds the animal, which causes it to be very careful ever afterwards in returning to a gāra; but in jungles where he has never been fired at in this way, he is less suspicious than the panther, which has an awkward habit of examining the trees adjacent to the carcase. The tiger sometimes takes the trouble of covering the kill with leaves, and in the case of a human victim killed when the sun is high, after drinking the blood he will carry the body to some shady spot, and use the clothing for that purpose.

Wolves are not often met with in the Mysore or Hyderabad (Deccan) country, although some years ago in the Central Provinces they became very bold, and were in the habit of entering villages and carrying off children. When oobāra shooting in Scinde, they were frequently seen; but they knew the range of a gun to a nicety, and never let the camel I was riding within eighty yards of them. On one occasion I tried to spear a wolf which passed close to me in the Neermul jungle one morning when on the line of march. He did not at first realise that he was being pursued, and I got to within thirty yards of him at the start; this distance, however, he kept throughout a long gallop, during which several spurts were made, when he increased his pace correspondingly, and seemingly without effort, and when I reined my horse up dead beat, he was still lobbing along at the same pace, and seeming to enjoy the fun. Instances are on record of wolves having been run down and speared, but they were probably handicapped by a heavy meal beforehand. They hunt in packs of about a dozen strong, and resemble the wild dog in their methods of hunting and general habits.

The wild dog* resembles a lanky collie in shape, the colour being a foxey red in the Annamullays, and a brownish-red further north and in the Central Provinces, both having a black tag to the brush. When in packs, as they generally are, they are very bold, and sometimes not only killed our haylas that had been tied up for tigers, but made way for us very reluctantly when we appeared on the scene. Our shikaries were very loth to inspect the kills on such occasions, stating that they would be attacked by the dogs, which feared nothing, not even tigers. They hunt in packs of about a dozen strong, and wherever they appear the jungles will be found to be denuded of game, from deer upwards. The natives all assert that when a tiger finds himself unexpectedly among wild dogs, he feigns to be dead, and they subject his body to various indignities; all shikaries of Southern India from the Central Provinces to the Annamullays, of every caste and creed, unanimously agree on this point. Their pups were not unfrequently brought for sale into Cantonments, but owing to an idea that their bite was invariably followed by hydrophobia, they never found a market.

At Bangalore a brother officer bought a young hyena, which grew up into a fine animal of its kind, and apparently became quite tame; until one morning, when playing with it, his foot became entangled in its chain and he fell to the ground, whereupon the affectionate brute sprang on him at once, biting him savagely; but an acquaintance who happened to be passing his compound heard the noise, and, rushing in, rescued him with the

* Cuon rutilans.

help of a heavy stick, with which he stunned the beast. Down in those parts it was always said that the taming of a hyena was impossible, and an encounter of this kind had been frequently predicted. For the benefit of the shikaries, who got a Government reward of five rupees for each, we occasionally shot these cowardly and revolting brutes, which are associated in my memory with a horrible scene which will not bear description; suffice it to say that they are veritable ghouls.

When in the Annamullays, a brother officer shot an immense python, or anaconda—I saw the skin, which he stated was 23 feet long when first removed. He was bison stalking at the time, and saw what he at first thought was the trunk of a tree lying on the ground, which presently began to move, whereupon the Carders bolted. He soon discovered its head, and put a bullet through it, which made the reptile so lively that he made tracks too. Next day he returned and cautiously followed up the broad trail which it had made as it had writhed along through grass and bushes, finding it dead some few hundred yards distant.

The Carders tell wonderful stories about the size of some of these snakes. I once got a young one—about twelve feet long—and had it for two years, during which time it grew about three feet. It was kept in a large box, and fed regularly on bandicoots,* of which it would eat three at a meal, and would then probably touch nothing for a fortnight. It was a cross-tempered pet, and repeatedly bit me severely; its power of constriction, too, was very unpleasant On two occasions I stepped over cobras without seeing them. One instance has been already related, the other occurred in Burmah when out snipe

* Large rats, three times the size of an English one.

shooting. My friend who was with me saw the reptile suddenly spring up at the edge of a small bund as I crossed He fired at once and killed it within a yard of me.

The Bangalore country was full of cobras. I shot three during my first day's florican shooting in the large grass slopes near Soubadors Chettrum. Strong gaiters to within a few inches of the knee render one practically safe. If bitten, there were two alternatives—to blow the piece out with the gun or to cut it out with a knife; there would then be some chance of life, but, otherwise, absolutely none. A dusky hamadryad once struck at me in Burmah; he was in a small box, and for some seconds I was not sure whether he had bitten me or not; luckily he missed his shot. This snake is allied to the cobra, and is a cannibal, eating his own tribe—death ensues about half an hour after being bitten. Many fatal cases occur among natives, but those among Europeans are extremely rare owing to their feet and legs being protected. There is a rather mythical creature named a bis-cobra, which the natives declare to be more deadly than the cobra. Those that have been pointed out to me were a smooth kind of lizard, striped with yellow, and snake-like in appearance, but of timorous nature, but they have the reputation of being aggressive at certain seasons, when their bite is said to be the precursor of immediate death.

Similar tales are extant of the large spider, so common in the bungalows, which the Tamil servants call a "jerry-mundlum." He is probably a species of "tarantula," but is, so far as my experience goes, a most harmless one.

With regard to aiming—head and neck shots being considered exceptional—the usual place with all animals is behind the shoulder blade and half way between the top of

TIGER'S HEAD.

SPOTTED DEER.
Span 23—length 29½ inches.

BROW-ANTLERED DEER.
Span 32—length 31¼ inches.
Brow Antlers, 14¾ inches.

SAMBUR.
Span 39¼ inches.
Right horn, 38¾ inches.
Left horn, 39⅝ inches.

BISON.

ELEPHANT'S FOOT.

SPECIMENS OF HORNS, ETC.

(Length Measurements taken from Coronets.

the withers and bottom of the girth. If the heart is missed the bullet penetrates the lungs, which, although not instantly fatal, is a deadly shot. If an animal is below you—a deer or ibex for instance—aim near the girth but not clear of the body; if he is above you, it is not in accordance with my experience that any allowance should be made, but some sportsmen say the point of aim should be higher. In all these cases the animal aimed at is supposed to be standing at ordinary sporting ranges; but, if moving, a proportional allowance must be made for distance, direction, and rate of speed. Practice alone will teach the amount, which with Express rifles is very small.

The following measurements of the heads of two bull bison are taken from one of my old diaries, and are the largest that appear in it, but the most symmetrical head measured about 33½ inches across the horns, and the upper portion is shown in the plate containing specimens of deers' heads.

Greatest breadth across horns, 39¾ inches; 38 inches.

Breadth from base to base of horns, 14 inches; 13½ inches.

Length from top of skull to nose, 19½ inches; 22½ inches.

CHAPTER XVI.

MISCELLANEOUS.

Neilgherry (or Nilgiri) Hills—Nunjengode—Shoot two alligators—Plucky fishermen — Nurseepoor—Another alligator—Woman's ring found in him—Adventure at Sacrabyle—Tulkaad—Sand drifts—More muggers—Small game—Shooting clothing—Babool dye—Sambur skin boots—Stalking shoes—Leggings—Spears—Boots—Nails and tent pegs—Arsenical soap—Pegging out skins—Golden rule—Rifles—Shells for—Detonating mixture—Malaria—Drinking water — Camp precautions — Smoking — Unhealthy seasons in jungles—Malarious spots—Quinine—Difficulty in obtaining tiger shooting—Good bags—Expenses—Soda-water—Liquors—Shooting grounds—Monsoon precautions—Tents—Black powder—Nitro powder—Conclusion.

Fever-stricken Tippicado, which is on the eastern confines of the great Wynaad forest, lies nearly midway between Mysore and Ootacamund, and is ten miles distant from the base of the Neilgherry Hills* at Seegoor. The travellers' bungalow at Bandipore is eight miles north of Tippicado, and is a more suitable spot for the sportsman, the malaria being less deadly than on the banks of the Moyaar. The road from Mysore to Ootacamund—seventy-eight miles in length—runs nearly due south the whole distance, crossing the Moyaar close to the bungalow at Tippicado. A few miles south of Goondulpett, at a

* An isolated mountain range about seventy miles south of Mysore city. It is thirty-five miles in length from east to west, and twenty-five in breadth. Ootacamund, its chief station, can also be reached *viâ* Metapolliam, on the Madras Railway.

distance of forty miles from Mysore, the road enters the outskirts of the jungle, near Gopaulswamy hill. This point is within twenty-four hours of Bangalore by rail and road, and within easy reach of the Chamraj Nugger jungles, and therefore favourably situated for shooting trips limited by short leave of absence.

In December, 1881, when shikaring in the Chamraj Nugger district, at the foot of the Billiga Rungum Hills, I received a letter from my friend Colonel Pearse, advising me to stay at Nunjengode, on the return journey to Mysore, to beat for a panther which had been doing a good deal of damage at that place, and to shoot some alligators in the Cubbany River, which ran close to the Maharajah's bungalow, in which I was to stay. This was situated in a park, and had formerly been a shooting lodge, the game in the vicinity being preserved by an ancestor of the present Maharajah. Accordingly, on my way back, I spent one day on the river, and shot two alligators, about 10 feet 6 inches long each, and wounded an immense brute as he lay basking on an island about 100 yards distant, but he got into a deep pool and was never seen again. The fishermen brought their nets and dragged the pool for his body, but could not find it. They were very plucky, and seemed to have no fear of being attacked by the alligators, stating that, for many years, nobody had ever been killed by them. From Nurseepore, eighteen miles off, however, news arrived of several people having been carried off by a mugger* which resided in a particular pool near that village. I had arranged to meet Pearse there the following day, so, leaving Nunjengode that night, I arrived there at 6 a.m., and pitched the camp in a shady tope of trees on the bank of the River Cauvery. While my breakfast was

* Alligator.

being prepared, I strolled down the river in pyjamas, with a local shikari, to have a look at the part where the alligator was reported to stay. It was a deep sullen pool at a bend of the river, about a quarter of a mile from camp, and which extended about seventy yards to a sand bank in the middle of the stream. On this bank, which was an island, the mugger was in the habit of basking every day. I went down the steep bank to the water's edge, and was looking for tracks when the shikari called me up, saying, "Come up, quick—the mugger will knock you into the water and kill you." On ascending, he explained that this brute was in the habit of knocking goats into the stream with his tail, when they were drinking, and then eating them, and that he had killed one the previous day in this manner. We proceeded further down the river to try the Express at some ruddy sheldrakes,* and on the way back to camp saw the alligator basking on the sand bank. Although they are lethargic brutes, they are often difficult to approach, and it is no easy task to get within 100 yards of them, but this one was successfully stalked, and at eighty yards' range I fired. His body immediately assumed a crescent shape, the head and tail being elevated, but he was too hard hit to leave the spot, and died in a few minutes. He was then towed ashore, and we had a post mortem on him, which resulted in a quantity of pebbles and a woman's toe ring being found in his stomach. The ring was promptly claimed by one of the villagers, who stated that it belonged to his wife, who had been carried off by this brute some three weeks previously.

This story was corroborated by some of those present, but the claim was withdrawn for three rupees, and the souvenir is now in my possession. This alligator was

* Or Brahmini duck—Casarea rutilans.

9 feet 8 inches long. The upper jaw is perforated by two holes, through which the canine teeth of the lower jaw enter, the ends appearing above the snout. The victim is seized by an arm or leg, and the alligator being dovetailed to it by this arrangement, has simply to use his weight to drown it, and can then devour it piecemeal at his leisure. On one occasion, having returned from a long day's beating for a tiger in the Sacrabyle jungles in Western Mysore, I strolled up the River Toonga for a dip, and, leaving my rifle and clothes on the bank, walked through some shallow water to a deep pool in the middle of the river. I was luxuriating in this, when the peon from the Travellers' Bungalow came running down, shouting, "Master, please come back; plenty big mugger got it." I lost no time getting into shallow water again, and before reaching the bank saw the log-like form of a huge mugger in the very spot I had been bathing not a minute previously. If he had meant business he could easily have seized me. Before my rifle could be reached he disappeared. The peon told me that this mugger had drowned a water buffalo a few weeks before my arrival by dovetailing on to its nose when it was drinking, and as he adhered to this story, in spite of a severe cross-examination, and had nothing to gain by telling a falsehood, I believed his statement to be a true one.

The day after the death of the Nurseepoor alligator, Colonel Pearse, Mr. Davy, and I, went to see Tulkaad village — eight miles distant on the left bank of the Cauvery. We waded across this river near a bend, where an immense accumulation of sand has been formed. During certain winds this sand is carried towards the village, which is gradually becoming submerged by these deposits. The sand drifts had already blocked three of the largest streets, and the tops of some full-grown Palmyra palms, just appearing over the surface, had a very novel effect. Three large temples had also been covered by the drifts, but it having been decreed by some Brahmin priests that, in order to stop an epidemic of cholera, it would be necessary to perform poojah in two of these edifices, a vast crowd had assembled a short time before our arrival, and, after immense labour, had excavated a passage to their interiors. The drifts on the side of the village nearest the river were nearly thirty feet high. The following days were devoted to more muggers; and some small game shooting, snipe being very plentiful in several places, Mr. Davy getting a bag of twenty brace in a few hours. For the hot weather the best dress for the jungle is a very loose cotton jacket, shaped like a shell jacket, stained light brown with the bark of the babool tree. Pockets are useless, and only catch in thorns, &c. Inside the jacket buttons must be sewn for a quilted cotton garment, which should invariably be worn during the day, as it protects the spine and liver from the intense rays of the sun. This is removable at pleasure, and for early morning or evening work can be unbuttoned and temporarily set aside, but it is an absolutely indispensable protection at other times. The headdress, whether helmet or sola (pith) topee, must be dyed the same colour as the jacket. A sufficient quantity of the babool bark—about as much as a quart measure will contain—is boiled in a chatty (earthen vessel), and the clothing is inserted until the proper shade has been attained. As the colour lightens after a few days' wear, the tint of the cloth should always be deeper than what is wished for, before it is removed from the dye. For breeches a cloth called "char soutee"* is best, being stronger and better suited for rough work, such as climbing and riding.

* Four-thread woven cloth.

A capital shikar cloth is made in the Bangalore jail, and can be obtained from any durzee* in those parts. It resembles the Lovat mixture of the Highlands, but is greener in tint, and therefore better suited for forest work, such as bison stalking; moreover, it does not change its colour when wet, and is on that account preferable to the Scotch cloth. Sambur skin boots are the best for hot weather wear, but are useless for wet jungles, where they speedily become like pulpy brown paper. For rocky ground indiarubber-soled tennis shoes are best. I always wore spring leggings, buckled at the top and bottom. They were easily put on, the spring caused them to retain their shape when wet, and they gave complete protection from snakes and thorns. A broad leather belt should be worn round the waist, to which a pouch holding fifteen rounds of ammunition must be attached. A shikar knife may also be carried if desired. This belt also acts as a sort of kummerbund.

When small game shooting a jacket with pockets will be necessary for cartridges. My spears were made either by Arnachellum, of Salem, or a famous maker at Aurangabad, whose name I forget. One rifle should always be in the sportsman's hands, the other being carried by a shikari. My rifle was never relinquished until the shikaries assured me there was no further chance of a shot, and very seldom even then. I only remember to have met with game on one occasion, when the shikaries were carrying both rifles.

During the monsoon, ordinary shooting boots are preferable to those made of sambur skin. The field boot is also a good pattern, it dispenses with leggings and is suitable for riding. A leather cartridge bag carried by the shikari will hold extra cartridges, a flask, a sandwich, and

* Tailor.

some smoking tackle. For night shooting I used a bit of moist cotton wool on which the heads of some wet matches had been rubbed. This was fixed close to the foresight—that was before the days of luminous paint, which ought to be the very thing for this purpose. About ten dozen long iron nails should be taken for pegging out skins, and some iron tent pegs will be found very useful for hard ground, plenty of arsenical soap for preserving the fleshy parts of the skin (nose, lips, and feet) will be necessary. Ordinary wood ashes are best for the broad surfaces, and a mixture of these with powdered alum should be well rubbed into the skins before they are dried, which is effected by pegging them out on the ground, hairy side downwards, in the shade of a tree. They must be tapped with a stick every half hour to prevent the white ants from attacking them. They must always be lifted at dusk and stowed in a place beyond the reach of jackals or village dogs, which prowl round camps at night and eat anything they can find.

The following is a good recipe for arsenical soap:—Powdered arsenic 2oz., camphor 5oz., powdered lime 2 drachms, salt of tartar 6 drachms; these must be set aside unmixed. Then take 2oz. of white soap, cut it into thin slices and put it into a saucepan with a little water over a slow fire; stir frequently, and when melted add the lime and salts of tartar, then the arsenic, and finally the camphor; let it simmer for a few minutes and then transfer to an air-tight jar. Turpentine is also very effective, and can be used in the absence of arsenical soap, or in combination with it if so desired.

A golden rule for all big game shikaries is to "make the most of your first shot, a better chance will seldom occur." The rifle I took to India in 1867 was a pin-fire

12-bore polygroove by a celebrated maker, but had two great defects which frequently placed me in danger, viz., the cartridge cases often jammed after discharge, and it could only burn 2½ drachms of powder. This absurd charge behind a hollow bullet (which was recommended by the maker) gave very little penetration.

After some experience I substituted spherical balls for these with better results, but much was still to be desired. I then had a 12-bore central fire polygroove made to order by Rigby, chambered to burn 7⅛ drachms of powder (Curtis and Harvey's No. 6 coarse grain), barrels 24 inches long. With 4 drachms powder and spherical bullets, it could put shot after shot from both barrels well into the centre of an 8-inch bull's-eye at 100 yards.

Behind shells, the charge used was 4½ drachms powder, and for bison and elephants 5½ and 7⅛ drachms respectively, with solid, hardened bullets. I have shot some tigers, panthers, bears, and a good many deer with a ·500 Express rifle, and in the majority of cases found it very effective; but it lacks penetration, owing to the bullet being too light, too much metal is lost by the size of the cavity; no rifle could drive such a projectile through a tiger's shoulder so as to reach the heart or lungs in a position which is not unfrequently offered to the sportsman, viz., a three-quarter shot facing you; indeed, with even a very small cavity, it is doubtful if any bullet from a sporting rifle can do so. The detonating mixture for shells was composed of equal weights of chlorate of potash and black antimony. This compound was not too sensitive, and never burst until the projectile had penetrated some inches; its effect was very marked, splinters of lead penetrating the softer tissues to a distance of nearly a foot from the seat of explosion. About 20 per cent. of these shells failed to explode;

but in these cases the projectile mushroomed out in the usual way, inflicting a severe wound. On my next trip I hope to use a ·577 Express for tigers, bears, panthers, &c., a double-barrel 8-bore rifle for the larger animals, and nothing can beat a ·450 Express for deer and antelopes, while in certain favourable positions it is quite powerful enough to kill a tiger.

The rutting season with sambur begins in October and November; the stags' antlers are then at their best, and as big game shooting in the plains cannot be then successfully followed, owing to the vast amount of long grass and other covert, the sportsman can employ his time with advantage in stalking these fine animals on the slopes of the Southern Indian hills. The jungles at the foot of these hills being very deadly at that season, had better be avoided; nor are they suited for stalking, except in the month of July, when many of the stags are in velvet, and consequently unfit to be shot. The sambur does not adhere to a grass diet alone; he is very partial to several kinds of jungle fruits of the plum tribe (as also are bison and elephants), and in many parts of the Neilgherries the orchards containing peach trees were much damaged by their inroads.

An old stag generally prefers to lie up for the day in a small sholah on commanding ground, near the centre of which he makes his form (like a hare's), and from which position he can detect the approach of all enemies. In the larger sholahs he is more at the mercy of the tiger and panther, who can stalk him with ease in the dense undergrowth. All deer, too, are fond of the pods of many kinds of trees, the babool, for instance, to eat which the antelope will travel many miles. Nice stalking will be obtainable in the month of March, when the pods are formed on these trees if they are in the vicinity of any plains resorted to by these animals. On shooting the male of any of the deer tribe, or ibex, the appendages should be immediately removed, as they affect the flavour of the venison. The skin of the sambur when tanned makes excellent leather for gaiters, boots, and shika belts. It will be sufficient to peg the skin out in the usual way, rubbing wood ashes and alum well in until it is quite dry, tanning operations being deferred until return to civilisation.

To guard against malaria—the greatest enemy the Indian sportsman has to contend with—a few grains of quinine should be taken daily before dinner, and all your followers should be similarly dosed.

In unhealthy jungles boil all water before drinking it—filtering it alone is insufficient; don't dig up the surface of the ground in camp; sleep at least three feet above the ground level, and higher still if it can be managed; always sleep under mosquito curtains; they keep off the breeze, but after a few days' basking in the sun one gets case-hardened and less sensitive to heat; moreover, the beds are always placed outside the tents at night.

During the rains calico curtains should be used in malarious districts, as they afford better protection than the ordinary gauze ones. A small fire at the door of the tent or hut is also very desirable during the monsoon. The rooms in some travellers' bungalows, which are situated in damp and unhealthy districts (Bandipore, for instance), are unprovided with fireplaces, which is a serious oversight. But, in spite of all precautions, the sportsmen can hardly escape getting fever in some jungles, the worst districts in this respect being generally the best for sport, as their evil reputation secures them immunity from all except the keenest sportsmen. It is therefore necessary to decide whether the sport is worth the risk—the fever is seldom fatal—and although in after years it may occasionally inconvenience one, but few sportsmen regret their original decision in the affirmative. Smoking is also a salutary habit in malarious jungles, and before leaving the tent or hut in the morning a cheroot or pipe should be lighted.

In different jungles the malaria varies according to the time of year in a very marked way, and shooting trips must be timed to avoid unhealthy periods. In the primeval forests, the unhealthy season lasts from the beginning of November to the beginning of July, whereas in jungles of the medium forest type, such as those of the Mahoor and Neermul * districts, the malaria is least from the beginning of March to the first rains in June, after which they become very feverish. The annual grass-burning operations are undoubtedly of great utility in checking malaria by diminishing the amount of vegetable matter, which by its decay engenders malaria.

It occasionally happens that a jungle of good repute plays a party false, and that the majority of its members are suddenly incapacitated by fever. A case of the sort occurred at Bangalore some years ago, when a party of three officers—who had been shikaring in the Billiga Rungums—were attacked by malignant fever, and obliged to return to Cantonments, only one of whom survived the illness. Even the Hyderabad jungles occasionally afford similar cases in the hot weather, and they must be attributed to bad drinking water, or unsanitary sites for camps, such as spots near old burial grounds or bottoms

* Or Nirmul—this district lies south of the Godavery, in the Nizam's dominions.

of valleys, near accumulations of stagnant water, where the shade afforded by trees frequently offers inducements which outweigh all sanitary considerations. It is certain, however, that a daily modicum of quinine modifies, if it fails to prevent, an attack of fever.

Unless quartered near parts of India where tigers are numerous, or acquainted with friends who will invite him to join their shooting parties, a beginner will probably find it difficult to bag even his first tiger. Of course, an unexpected opportunity of doing so may occur; but even twenty-five years ago, when they were more numerous than at present, I spent three months in the jungles before shooting my first tiger, previous to which nearly fifty hard days in the sun had been spent in unsuccessful beats.

The best bag I ever remember to have been made at Secunderabad, was that in the hot weather of 1871, which amounted to thirty-one tigers, and over fifty panthers and bears, the average number of rifles being eight; but several of the sportsmen were unable to get more than one month's leave, and changes consequently occurred at intervals throughout that period.

The best bag made by a small party was that by Captains Broadhurst, Thorneycroft, and Travers in 1884, who, in the Godavery district, shot twenty-four full-grown tigers and three bears in two and a half months, and caught two tiger's cubs and two young bears in addition. Their largest tiger measured 10 feet from tip of nose to tip of tail along the curves. Captain Thorneycroft, of my regiment, shot an exceptionally large tigress which measured 9 feet 2½ inches along the curves. Major Mansel Pleydell, 12th Lancers, was also a very successful sportsman, killing forty-four tigers to his own rifle during a comparatively short term of service in the Deccan extending over a few years. Three of these tigers were man-eaters, for one of which he received a reward from the Mysore Government of Rupees 300. On two occasions he shot four tigers to his own gun in two days. Only one tiger out of the forty-four was over 10 feet in length. Major Pleydell was a keen sportsman and spared no expense to ensure good sport, his arrangements being perfect, and his shikaries the best at Secunderabad.

The expenses of a tiger shooting trip average about 350 rupees a month for each individual of a party of three guns, exclusive of liquor. If there are more members the expenditure decreases in proportion to their numbers, the heaviest items being payments for beaters and for gāras by tigers. Whenever a tiger was shot the beaters got double pay, viz., 4 annas apiece; as 120 were generally employed, the amount expended came to only Rupees 30 for the day's work. The outlay for gāras came to about Rupees 250 per mensem. This included small presents for the use of the haylas as baits, viz., about 4 annas per diem apiece. Of these we had never less than one dozen, and sometimes as many as thirty tied up, so that the total amount for beaters and gāras exceeded Rupees 500 per mensem.

Soda-water is an absolute necessity in the jungle in hot weather. Large quantities must be taken out, and arrangements must be made to send back the empties and to obtain fresh supplies periodically. Nothing is so refreshing as soda-water when drunk from the bottle so as to imbibe as much as possible of the gas. No other liquor except water should ever be taken while under arms during the day; cold tea soon ferments and becomes nauseating, nor is it possible to keep it cool. Claret and hock mixed with soda-water, and an occasional glass of beer, will take the place of stronger drinks in camp, spirits becoming distasteful after one has been exposed to the sun, but some brandy and champagne should always be available in case of need.

A grand field for sport exists in that vast expanse of mountain and forest, stretching over one hundred miles in a south-westerly direction, from Denkanicotta (forty miles south-east of Bangalore), to Danaikencotta, which is situated in the valley of the Moyaar, twenty miles west of the junction of that river with the Bowani. This tract extends from Collegal on the north, nearly to Erode, a distance of sixty miles in a southerly direction, and comprises the valleys of the Moyaar, the Bowani, and the Cauvery, with their tributaries, together with several hill ranges, chief of which are the Billiga Rungums,* and the Hona Mattys, the former consisting of three parallel ranges, which run nearly north and south, from the Cauvery to within twenty miles of the Neilgherries, the Hassanoor Ghaut being close to their southern extremity, and which are thirty miles in length by ten in breadth. The western range of these hills is in Mysore, the two others being in the Coimbatore district, British territory. The Hona Mattys are close to the Billiga Rungums, and consist of two ridges, each thirty-five miles in length, and ten in breadth; they are uninhabited, and almost unknown to any shikari. At their south-eastern extremity lies Guddysal—a good camping ground. These magnificent forests contain every kind of Southern Indian game except ibex and buffalo. All this area is bounded on the south by the Bowani, which receives the waters of the Moyaar—formed by the northern watershed of the Neilgherries—at Sattimungalum, and thence flows eastwards, until it joins the

* White rock mountains.

Cauvery near Erode, a station on the Madras railway. This would form a convenient point of departure, and one at which it would be easy to obtain supplies and transport, or if preferred a start might be made from the northern side, either from Bangalore or from Mysore, the latter for choice, as bases for supply are more numerous at the foot of the hills in that direction, and the operations would not necessitate crossing the Cauvery. The discomforts of camping during the monsoon would have to be faced, at which season only can these jungles be entered with comparative safety; but all disagreeable experiences should be effaced by the good sport which ought to be obtained in the course of such a trip. The Annamullay and Travancore hills, which extend from the village of the former name nearly to Cape Comorin, the southernmost point of India, over a tract of country two hundred miles in length, and varying from fifteen to forty miles in breadth, is also a possible hunting ground that should not be forgotten, and one where the ibex will be found on the higher peaks, some of which attain an elevation of nearly 9000 feet above the sea. Either the village of Annamullay, or that of Cochin, in Travancore, would form the best starting point. The Pulney Hills lie about forty miles south-east of Annamullay village, and also afford good sport including some ibex shooting. For monsoon work, be careful to take waterproof covers for the rifles, and ground sheets for every individual of the party. Tents for a hot weather trip should always include a hill tent, with double fly, for refuge during the heat of the day, A good one can generally be picked up for Rupees 250, this with a bechoba and a rowtee, should suffice for a party of three guns.

A bechoba costs about Rupees 100, and is light and commodious, and when pitched under trees, such as the mango and peepul, affords sufficient protection from the sun's rays. A rowtee for the use of the servants costs Rupees 60. For shooting in remote jungles, where coolies are scarce and no other transport is available, the Regulation single pole bell tent, conical in shape, and which can be carried by two men, is everything that can be desired for a solitary sportsman. Accommodation can be supplemented by the construction of huts if necessary.

In the sheltered valleys of these forests, on a damp, muggy day in the monsoon, the smoke of black powder hangs terribly, enveloping the firer in an opaque cloud, which not only prevents him from seeing the effect of his shot, but is very likely to give a clue to a wounded animal as to his position.

In jungles where bison have seldom been harassed by sportsmen, they undoubtedly often mistake the report of firearms for thunder, which is prevalent at the breaking of the monsoon, and for a month afterwards, this too, being the usual time for stalking. On several occasions I have fired at a bison without disturbing the remainder of the herd, who would merely start on hearing the report, but recommence grazing immediately afterwards. Native shikaries also assert that tigers and panthers which have been fired at, and missed, over a kill at night, often return to it after a few minutes, mistaking the flash and report for lightning and thunder. Whenever a waterproof nitro powder is invented which can be used in large charges without danger of detonation, it will entirely supplant black powder for shooting in heavy jungles.

On account of the difficulty in keeping cartridges dry, when under canvas, during the rains, and the tendency of paper cases to swell when damp, thereby impeding rapid loading, it will be desirable to use only those in which the paper portion is enclosed in a brass cylinder.

Several chapters on small game shooting in Scinde, the Deccan, and Burmah were compiled from my diaries with a view to publication in this volume, which, however, has already exceeded its contemplated proportions, and must now be brought to a close, with apologies for its imperfections.

INDEX.

G.

H.

I.

T.